HORIZON

SUMMER, 1966 · VOLUME VIII, NUMBER 3

Some Aspects of Modernization

More than any other person Nathaniel Hawthorne is responsible for our mind's-eye image of early New England. From our reading of his works, in any case, most of us tend to recall his preoccupation with the dark and gloomy areas of Puritan life, with the ghost-infested fabric of ancient houses. Yet, in his greatest novel, *The Scarlet Letter*, as R. V. Cassill observes in his article beginning on page 32, Hawthorne was actually as much concerned with the abiding problems of human psychology as he was with the grim moral codes of his New England antecedents. And as for the old houses, Hawthorne elsewhere suggested that he would willingly have seen them burned to rid the scene of their baleful haunts. In *The House of the Seven Gables*, indeed, he envisioned a point in the future where, to escape the dead hand of the past, each generation would build for itself its own homes, its own offices, and its own public structures.

Fortunately—as we see it—the House of the Seven Gables itself still stands in Salem, as does the Old Manse in Concord, where Hawthorne lived when he was first married—and, barring accident, they will no doubt survive for years to come. Other buildings possessing more or less historic interest and architectural distinction have not fared as well, especially in our rapidly changing and growing cities. In an article on landmark preservation (pages 48–59) Roger Starr refers to the large numbers of such structures that have been demolished and deformed throughout the nation over the past quarter-century. How to preserve what is left of this diminishing architectural heritage is causing highly charged concern at every level of our society, from local neighborhoods to the office of the President. Mr. Starr himself views the situation not only with an informed appreciation of the architectural past but with concern for the needs of the present and the future. At times, he points out, there is a conflict between these considerations that does not favor the preservation of landmarks, however hallowed these may seem to be in the eyes of preservationists.

Many of us would be less disturbed by the destruction of certain old buildings if we had any assurance that their replacements, however modern in style and character, would have some

HORIZON is published every three months by American Heritage Publishing Co., Inc.

PRESIDENT
James Parton

EDITOR-IN-CHIEF
Joseph J. Thorndike

EDITORIAL DIRECTOR, HORIZON
Oliver Jensen

EDITORIAL DIRECTOR, BOOK DIVISION
Richard M. Ketchum

ART DIRECTOR
Irwin Glusker

Editorial and executive offices: 551 Fifth Avenue, New York, N.Y. 10017.

EDITOR
Marshall B. Davidson

MANAGING EDITOR: Ralph Backlund   ART EDITOR: Jane Wilson

ART DIRECTOR: Elton Robinson

ASSOCIATE EDITORS: Shirley Tomkievicz, Norman Kotker

ASSISTANT EDITORS: Barbara Klaw, Wendy Buehr

EDITORIAL ASSISTANT: Priscilla Flood

COPY EDITOR: Mary Ann Pfeiffer   *Assistant:* Joan Wilkinson

ADVISORY BOARD: Gilbert Highet, *Chairman*, Frederick Burkhardt, William Harlan Hale, Jotham Johnson, John Walker

EUROPEAN CONSULTING EDITOR: J. H. Plumb, *Christ's College, Cambridg*

EUROPEAN BUREAU: Gertrudis Feliu, *Chief, 11 rue du Bouloi, Paris Ier*

Horizon
A Magazine of the Arts

SUMMER, 1966 · VOLUME VIII, NUMBER 3

equivalent architectural merit. It is only one of the paradoxes of our affluent Great Society that the nature of the buildings we live and work in becomes increasingly determined by factors of economy and utility—what too often emerges as the starkness of "contractor's modern." The built-in obsolescence of such structures may yet lead us, if by different reasoning, to the systematic renewals envisioned by Hawthorne.

The highly decorative illustration at left represents the device of Youssouf Bey, a top-ranking diplomat of the Ottoman Empire, some of whose brilliant caricatures enliven pages 24–31 of this issue. As far as we can determine, this is the first time these intimate graphic commentaries on life "inside Constantinople" during the 1880's and '90's—or anything quite like them—have been published. They are selected from a large, leatherbound album discovered a few years ago almost by chance in a Turkish antique shop and since brought to this country. The caricature is a European art form. These consummately realized examples not only provide fresh evidence of the early westernization of Turkey; they also reveal some of the inner secrets of Ottoman diplomacy in dealing with the aggressive demands of European powers. Here, as is often the case, art speaks to us when histories remain dumb. THE EDITORS

COVER: *Le Mezzetin*, a slightly cropped reproduction of which appears on our cover, was painted by Jean Antoine Watteau shortly before his untimely death. This small canvas probably represents a friend, dressed in a costume owned by the artist, as one of the stock characters of the *commedia dell' arte*. The painting was acquired by Watteau's patron Jean de Jullienne and later, in 1767, by Catherine the Great. In 1934 it was sold by the Soviet Union and is now one of the treasures of the Metropolitan Museum of Art (Munsey Fund).

Must she be made to seem, as recent fashions picture her, like a preadolescent girl,

a willful little boy,

IMPORTED ITALIAN VELVETEEN ENSEMBLE
BY JACK WINTER

4

Whatever Has Become of Mommy?

By AGNES DE MILLE

On the theory that children were at most imperfect or unfinished adults, and were therefore bound to fault all situations until old enough to behave with grown-up discretion, they were long dressed as miniature men and women and not as children at all. Their special needs and comforts were never accommodated. It was hoped that if their passing regrettable condition were ignored, they would be encouraged to stamp out all childish traits—with the single exception of innocence, which they were bound to lose in any case.

Childish traits were otherwise defined as ignorance, willfulness, selfishness, and foolishness—in short, the whole gamut of human failing, saving only sexuality. It was felt that sexuality was the prime grown-up short-coming, and children were paid the compliment of being treated as neuters. With this in mind, they were packaged indistinguishably, wrapped tight and bound, leaving only the head visible and the eyes and gaping mouth movable. Thus fettered, they were often strapped to a board and carried on the mother's back or hung up on the wall. And this custom, although perhaps a deterrent to the development of individual expression, was in many ways pleasant for the babies, for it kept them safe and companionably present in all family fun. It also kept them free from temptation, sexual or otherwise, which was the purpose of the practice.

Swaddling persisted in Europe throughout the Renaissance and Reformation up to the end of the eighteenth century. Even today in a modern country like Japan, a child is carried on the back of a near relative until well past walking age. I have a memory of a four-year-old tied to his ten-year-old brother, enjoying a baseball game. Brother came up to bat wearing his sibling, a kimono, and high wooden getas.

There being no parlor way of differentiating the sex of toddlers, boys and girls continued, after release from infant bands, to proclaim their similarity by dressing alike, and since they were constrained to the imitation of grown-ups, it was necessarily the imitation of a single parent. This turned out to be, oddly enough, the female parent.

Perhaps the choice was thought to accentuate innocence, girls being obviously purer than boys; perhaps the choice was thought less harmful to boys than the reverse would have been for girls. Perhaps it was unconscious

r, well—whatever?

DRAWINGS BY MICHAEL RAMUS

PHOTO MARC HISPARD—*Queen*; CAMERA PRESS FROM PIX

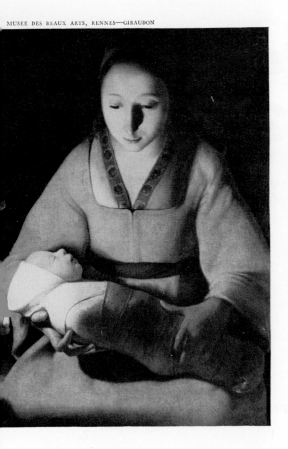

Georges de La Tour's Newborn Child (left) *shows a seventeenth-century baby tightly swaddled into a state of compulsory innocence. In New England later in the same century, young Henry Gibbs* (right), *going on two, dressed like his sister Margaret* (farther right) *and in the image of Mommy until he grew up a bit. A detail from Watteau's* La Danse (opposite page, right) *and a portrait by Pierre Mercier* (extreme right) *show an eighteenth-century preadolescent girl and boy elegantly dressed in exactly the same style as their female and male parents.*

desire on the part of the mother to assert domination in the short time allotted her for the care of her son. Girls stayed beside their mothers until marriage, but boys in previous centuries were separated from the women and taken over by the men while still very young.

If while still under their mother's influence the young males minded being dressed as little women, if they felt it cast a blight on their virility, they never said. The rich ones developed a taste in fancy furbelows which they were never asked to relinquish, and they flaunted and ruffled their way through wars, explorations, sinkings, sackings, and martyrdoms in creations that would make Seventh Avenue gasp. Contrary to what we might suppose, they were not a whit less adventuresome or frightening for their frills and feathers. Indeed, they gained stature through them. For long after bodily decoration ceased to be ritualistic, it continued to serve as the mark of class and rank, and in fact became so essential to the maintaining of social position that prerogative in dress was protected by law. Ermine was reserved for the king, flowing hair for the aristocrats. Certain colors, furs, and materials were likewise restricted to the nobility, and if economics did not guarantee sanctions, royal edict did.

It was the English Puritans who first embraced the limitations of lower-class dress as a badge of honor, voluntarily cutting their hair (The Roundheads) and adopting sober homespun and clean white starch as the mark of their dedication and the discipline of their democracy.

From the Puritans, the American middle-class man took his color (which was drab), as well as from New World hunters and soldiers (which, for practical purposes concerning available dye and the need for camouflage, tended to be subdued). Our responsible citizens today still dress in the spirit of Puritans or of seventeenth-century foot soldiers and farmers.

But fancy as many a gentleman or warrior might be, he never dressed like a woman except as a disguise or a carnival prank. No plumed and curled courtier wore skirts—and no lady wore pants. It was an open scandal if any did, and the clergy merely voiced overwhelming popular opinion on this matter. The Church burned Joan of Arc partly because she wore men's hose and would not return to women's clothing, her transvestitism being considered the livery of the devil and a sure sign of witchcraft.

Yet notwithstanding the careful sexual distinction in dress for adults, the odd sexual confusion in dress for children continued. Whether aristocratic or humble, boys for centuries dressed as girls until they were breeched. Thereafter they dressed in the exact style of their fathers. If aristocrats, the little boys wore velvet and satin even for romping, and were curled or powdered and peruked; if yeomen, farmers, craftsmen, or artisans, they were clipped short and coated in wool and leather. Similarly, small gentlewomen wore their mama's petticoats, stockings, heeled shoes, pierced ears, stays, powdered hair,

BRUCKMANN—GIRAUDON · LORD FARINGDON

rouge, and patches. Small servants wore matronly caps and aprons. A farm child's skirts were long to the ankle; a little lady's trailed the floor. In all cases the girls' hair, whether from high or low born scalps, was soon up, for a daughter was never so much a child in her own right as she was a promise. There was a great need for early and continuous breeding, as a result of plagues and wars, and a girl had to be about her business early. Hopefully, she was to be married and bearing as soon as she was biologically able, because she was very likely not going to live to be thirty. In the case of dynastic unions, marriage contracts were often sealed at birth to make sure.

Girlhood was obviously not carefree or frivolous, and for the young female there was to be no nonsense about kicking up her heels, or rolling on the grass, or climbing and jumping like her brother. Her disciplining consisted mainly of teaching her a few domestic skills and of breaking her of any wild or hoydenish instincts. She was weighted down, hooped, and hobbled; she was abjured, exhorted, warned. Above all, she was trained in obedience and in restraint of self-will. Boyish freedom would not further her career as a woman, and womanly it was her decreed fate to be; that, or worse than nothing.

Outside of riding and walking, accordingly, there were no athletics for ladies, and outside of dancing there was no vigorous recreation. Little servants used up their energy in drudgery. Little ladies let off high spirits with tops and shuttlecocks, dollies and embroidery frames.

Urgent destiny was kept constantly in mind, not only through her dress but in her deportment and manners. Whatever she did, she stood and sat with her feet together, crossing only her ankles. She kept her eyes downcast and her hands quiet and clasped. She did not raise her arms, let alone her legs, and the effect she made was of a creature special, precious, and vulnerable, a creature designed for female purposes, reserved, set aside and waiting until the great mysteries took over, when she would became of value. As a person in her own right she barely counted until pubescence. Then the long skirts and low neckline she was already wearing became her proper uniform. She did not need to modify her costume; she merely took possession of it. She was now marriageable and her flag was flying.

Her brother's rights changed even more radically, although his suits, like his sister's clothes, altered only in size. But as he began to shave he began also to handle a sword or a gun, and not as toys. His sports had to do with self-defense and procuring food, and they were in deadly earnest. He was sent off to college or the army, or put to a trade, or he was married straightaway. For him, also, childhood—which had barely begun—was entirely over.

The nineteenth century saw changes, possibly because life expectancy was by then a little greater. Infants, while no longer swaddled, were still overdressed. They began, however, to enjoy some concessions as to age and sex.

PHOTO ALICE AUSTEN; STATEN ISLAND HISTORICAL SOCIETY

In 1886, properly dressed and picturesquely arranged about the branches of a sumac, Mrs. Cocroft of Staten Island and her ten children ("born as close together as nature would permit") quietly posed for a camera. A contemporary Mom (at right), as casually breeched and sandaled as both her son and daughter, cavorts with the freedom of a male athlete.

KEN HYMAN—MERIDIAN

The boy's hair was cut when he was put in pants, at five or six; the girl's skirts shortened when she started to walk and kept at the knee until adolescence. Drawers, a garment which an eighteenth-century woman would have looked on as superfluous, were adopted as a decent necessity under the transparent Empire dresses. They were never afterward to be discarded. To the drawers were soon added ankle-length pantalettes, and the legs that were exposed under the first knee-length skirts were thereafter modestly hidden. But pantalettes were a feminine garment in no way resembling brother's trousers; there was to be no suggestion that sister was taking up male clothing. They were frilled, embroidered, and scalloped, and might be of the finest muslin—but they were always opaque. However, because she wore them, sister could now lift her legs a bit and romp with a modicum of freedom, but she was enjoined to do this daintily and circumspectly.

It was not until the close of the nineteenth century that girls first began actually to dress like boys. About 1890 they were put into "rompers" for playing, one-piece suits with baggy-knee bloomers. At a slightly older age they wore belted one-piece dresses and smocks, but kept the bloomers which obviated the tyranny of petticoats. Boys also wore smocks or long-skirted suits and bloomers. They were called Buster Brown suits. Both boys and girls began also to wear sport suits and bathing costumes, although girls retained long stockings and sleeves.

The differences have diminished steadily over the years. Today, as before, infants are still dressed alike in a kind of unlabeled package, but at toddling time girls now follow their brothers—that is, they are both breeched instead of petticoated, and they tend both to be shorn. Their toys are for the most part identical. She still plays with dolls, and he does not scorn to also, although he has his own. Anything he plays with she shares, and—except on very formal occasions—anything he wears. In playgrounds, grade schools, high schools, and colleges, boys and girls tend to dress almost identically, in dungarees, sweat shirts, pull-overs, socks, and sneakers—very nearly impossible to tell apart even as to size. General scruffiness is the accepted style. The confusion and casualness stop short only at the door of the church or in places of formal courtship.

The change began just after World War I. The girl-child of the twenties began wearing skirts which barely covered her thighs. She was for the first time in the Christian Era bare-armed and barelegged. She was shapeless, her dress hanging like a sack from the neck, and the impression she made was as sexless as that of an insect.

In all this her mother astonishingly reversed the process of history and began to imitate the daughter. Mama's skirts were above the knee, her dresses were straight shifts, her belts, if any, were low on her tight, boyish thighs. Her waist was obliterated, as well as her hips and her bust. Young girls actually strapped themselves flat in an effort to break down and reduce mammary tissue. On any but the slimmest of bodies these pillow slips hung wrinkled like prison garments; and when hips and bust defied concealment and bulged unwanted, the eye was teased away from the unlovely protuberances by bits of trailing chiffon, long beads, or flowers at shoulder or hip. The asexual effect was further heightened by a drastic cropping of hair, even to the shaving of the nape; both old and young deprived themselves eagerly of the tresses that had been from the beginning of recorded history the pride of the grown woman. Not since the fifteenth century, when the public display of female hair was forbidden by church fiat, have women submitted to such penitential cutting.

The preferred stance for modeling this monastic coiffure and garment was a kind of backward slant—or, alternatively, a slouch or a droop. In this posture it was impossible to tell what any female had or had not by way of natural endowments, large or small. Posture naturally dictated expression, and the prevalent expression was one of boredom. The fashionable woman not only looked like a little girl, but like a *sick* little girl—languid, listless, and unwilling.

This costume of the twenties was probably the ugliest, least provocative, least feminine, and most neurotic style of dressing the world has ever seen.

The men, on the other hand, remained more or less as they had been, fiddling about with details of appearance, but otherwise basically unchanged.

Both sexes, however, had begun to throw off clothing with an extreme lack of caution. Nakedness had heretofore been the prerogative of children. Adults want to cover themselves, and the urgency to do this had seemed the very essence of maturity. But now that women were dressing as girl-children, they dropped all adult protective differentiation. The long, exposed legs were bare or flesh-colored. The arms and shoulders were unveiled, and —for the very first time—the armpits! For, except among people who habitually go naked to the waist, the underarm has never been exposed. The subsequent steady progress toward nudity brought about what is perhaps the most childish characteristic of all: total abandonment of mystery. (In certain San Francisco restaurants waitresses currently serve lunch or dinner in topless bathing suits. I am told the style is a deterrent to appetite.) Women hitherto have found it effective to suggest much, to reveal little, to promise only. But they now show exactly what they have to offer with a reckless assurance that is either arrogance or, possibly, indifference. (Did not Harry Golden point out the basic relation between clothing and self-respect—and the effectiveness of breaking pride by forcing the inmates of concentration camps to go stark naked?)

It is true that today women are more beautiful than they ever were. With basic afflictions corrected, fat curbed, and peripheral blemishes smoothed away, age itself has been halted in its tracks. And a woman can go bare-skinned without becoming either a warning or a social nuisance. But in the casting away of modest veiling something has been lost, and it is a valuable and charming form of coquetry. The teasing these days tends to be outrageously provocative. Have men grown so jaded, then, that they need to be shocked into activity? This would be an expected result of the prevalent undressing.

These drastic changes occurred within forty years (it once took a hundred years to alter the shape of a hat), and coincided exactly with the social emancipation of women. Women were advertising their freedom from legal and political discrimination, from economic dependence, from moral stricture, from the slavery of perpetual childbearing, from all types of subservience and underprivilege. But these triumphs were none of their own doing, and the celebration was for victories won by others—by mothers and grandmothers. It was a time for wallowing in irresponsibility, for daring anything with adolescent bravado; women were enjoying freedom such as their sex had never known. And they were pretty vociferous about their new estate—and just as attractive as most people are in a picket line. These women dressed like their daughters because they wished to be like their daughters—and, what is very much to the point, they were able to be. Their grandmothers had made it possible.

The twenties was a period unfortunately followed by world-wide economic depression and world-wide war. These catastrophes gave pause to happy female progress, but not for long. No matter how terrible and sobering the event, people tend to resume their basic emotional development directly punishment is over. Women have seen no reason to abandon the prewar point of view regarding age, and today they continue to work their way steadily backward toward babyhood.

In previous centuries such conduct would have been considered unpardonably light-minded, if not downright witless, but it must be remembered that childhood in our time is pleasant where before it was not. For one thing, it used to be dangerous. The chances of survival were slim, the chances of approbation negligible. It was a time to be got through quickly. Now it is altogether safer and jollier, and everyone seems to hanker after the delights of early adolescence. Women of sixty speak of themselves as "girls," women of fifty as "dolls." Recognition of age is an insult, assumption of youth the highest flattery— just as though childbearing were still a woman's only economic warranty, and as though sexual attraction and enjoyment terminated at forty. Both are untrue, we know; yet the worship of perpetual childishness is a dominating feature of our time.

The confused relation between adult and child is reflected in contemporary toys. Although there are doll babies that blink and cry and wet and even, in luxurious types, throw up, there are equally desirable mannequins —the Barbie dolls—with bosoms (no nipples), waists, hips, calves, and complete wardrobes of snappy creations: spike-heeled sandals which can be put on and off, sunglasses, plastic handbags, make-up kits, mink stoles, diamond slave bracelets, all kept in superb luggage. Does the baby girl take this Las Vegas beauty to bed with her when darkness approaches? Or does she suck the corner of an old blanket that will remind her of Mommy in her less gorgeous but more cuddly moments?

Little brother also has his dolls, eighteen-inch G.I. Joes with "twenty movable parts" and suits and uniforms to put on and off, scuba suits, astronaut outfits, commando costumes, marine uniforms—with all their lethal accoutrements. There is even a doll decked out for jungle warfare in an expensive ready-made loincloth and head rag. These are not the equivalent of the old-fashioned lead soldier; they are mannequins to be dressed, undressed, cradled, and carried about—not, to be sure, in a bassinet or perambulator, but in a tiny yellow life-raft that also serves as a baby rest so that Buster can have his dream substitute nestling on his shoulder as he accompanies Mommy to the supermarket.

Dolls used to serve little girls for the training of maternal disciplines and habits, and for the learning of real household skills such as plain sewing. It was on her doll clothes that a girl learned to seam, French-seam, hem, gather, placket, buttonhole, hemstitch, featherstitch, bind, and French-roll. No more. Barbie and G.I. Joe come with machine-made wardrobes and need no mothering. They are substitute dream figures whom the child identifies only with the play (or fighting) aspects of adulthood, never with the basic parent-child functions. Here the infant is creating, not its own offspring, but its own parent. This is not surprising, since the parent has in many aspects become a child and joins gladly in the game of cross substitution.

Consider, for example, the cult of "look alikes"—garments for mother and daughter, hair-styling, accoutrements, fake jewelry, shoes, and make-up all the same. Together mother and progeny deny the generations and become siblings. There transpires a meeting midway between the ages: the child growing quaintly mature, the mother unnaturally young, in a curious mirror image achieved by double compromise. If the mother is wearing far less than she ever did before, the daughter borrows back from mother her own stolen nakedness—complete with mature sexual teasers which on her become irrelevancies, such as the fancy brassière tied across her undeclared chest. The approximation is accomplished with no

thought of forcing the little girl toward maturity as in older times, but of preserving, if not forever as long as possible, the parent's youth.

The mother figure has all but disappeared—the deep-bosomed earth woman, the madonna, the Queen Goddess. In her place Diana—the chaste huntress, the divine adolescent, the untouchable, the unchangeable—stands among her votaries and sisters (who are daughters) and among her brothers and hunters (who are her sons).

For the hallmark of our age—and it is a new one—is that when mother is not dressed like little daughter, she is dressed like little son. She wears trousers more often than not. She wears tunics that hide her figure, disguise her breasts, and erase her waist, shapeless sweaters, pullovers and parkas, sneakers and sandals. Everything is done to minimize the adult anatomy. The ideal legs are held to be long and lean in the calf like a male runner's, the ideal hips tight and slim, the ideal breasts small and high. As with men, it is the bones of the head, and the thighs, legs, hips, and groin that are emphasized. Not all women can achieve the effect of stalwart fitness, but all women seem to want to. And most garments are now designed to help. The whole body is kept sleek, firm, stripped, and ready.

For what? Why, for the chase! In the interests of unremitting sexual teasing, Mama has adopted the body of a hermaphrodite.

It is always possible to read back from gesture and stance, as well as from clothes, the psychology that prompts each.

Sir Alex Guinness once said that when a young man, he made a practice of imitating the mannerisms, the walk, and the gestures of prospective employers—and that once he could reproduce a set of physical characteristics, he would know all that he needed to know about the man who was interviewing him. If we were to imitate the posture of the models in our better fashion magazines, we would discover much that is illuminating. Here we stalk, splay-legged, mouth wide, stiff-armed and stretching; here we stand feet spread, arms akimbo; there we lie waiting, knees up, knees parted, feet in air.

The woman of the twenties and thirties drooped and slouched. Our girl of the sixties gapes and spreads. She is wide open, exposed, void of mystery.

The fashion photographers no doubt think to find good copy in such poses, and no one can deny that they are indeed both startling and new. From time immemorial, in every culture, in every race and class, woman through her fertile years has hidden and protected the source of her fertility as man has advertised his. Woman must do this because she is vulnerable. But today she is no longer vulnerable—contraceptives have altered this prime fact of life.

It would be easy to say that today women are imitating

Just before a crisis, women tend to follow opulent fashions, as the large-hatted, beplumed, ample-bosomed, tight-waisted, bell-skirted Edwardian belle at far left magnificently demonstrates. In postcrisis periods simpler, less mature modes take over. The bustless, hipless, short-skirted, bare-armed, generally girlish example in the center dates from the years following World War I. In this current year of dubious grace after World War II, Yves St. Laurent has come up with an abbreviated, straight-hanging, all-but-transparent "gown" revealing the woman who dons it as a girl-child, self-assured of— or, perhaps, arrogantly indifferent to—her sex characteristics.

men, but this is not precisely true. The currently fashionable trend may not be traditionally female, but at the same time it is not traditionally male. Neither adolescent boys nor grown men stand this way, unless by chance they are carrying guns, whips, or knives, or possibly tennis rackets or bats—unless, in short, they are getting into position for a fight. In showing us all how to be lovely, our fashion-magazine beauties are not so much imitating gentlemen as sensual, aggressive rapscallions. Fashion models, screen babes, and "Playmates" have taken on the stance of the street corner, the corral, the beachhead—or, if you prefer, the brothel, the dive, the fish market. Brutality has become titillating.

Why do models do this? Obviously, because they are told to and are paid up to fifty dollars an hour for obliging. The attitudes reflect the taste of dress designers and photographers, many of whom seem to prefer girls who look like bad little boys to girls who look like women. The models are apparently not quite bright enough to catch on to what is being done to them, or else the money is sufficient to persuade them to keep quiet.

But what about the customer? She has no need to please the photographer when she buys; she just wants to look adorable. Does her husband, then, find her endearing in these attitudes and costumes? Do her children? Whatever has become of Mommy?

These acrid strictures do not apply to *couturiers* like

Mainbocher and his very few peers—great artists who design beautiful, durable clothes which, because of their classic lines and workmanship, remain long in fashion. Fine craftsmen do a great deal for the grace and style of our time. They hold the line of good taste within a small group of wealthy clients, but they cannot check history. It is unlikely that Mainbocher has ever included a pair of pants in any of his collections, or any other defacing eccentricity. But he is in a minority—ladies' trousers are being manufactured by the millions.

History races in peculiar channels and not always where the ladies intend. The majority of women no longer make nor design their own clothes nor invent and execute trimmings as they once did. They buy what is offered them, ready-made, and while they will not buy what they detest, they can be teased and persuaded against instinct to an almost imbecile degree. The fashion industry in the United States is organized to do just this, and foists upon them en masse the ideas of a very small group, and not by any means the most tasteful group. Fashions now change in a period of months, where before they took decades. They are planned to render obsolete anything bought three months earlier. They are planned more than half a year in advance, and nothing short of war could stay their fulfillment. So if the uniform of the child-tyrant hangs on the racks of every store—and very little else is available—this is what is bought. It would take a persistent and courageous individualist, a woman with consider-

able time and energy, to flout this overpowering influence.

It can be stated categorically, however, that no fad endures for long unless the masses have some desire to co-operate—and so, to a degree, fashion does always speak for the wearer. Freak fashions may appear and disappear like reflections on water, but there are certain stable characteristics that last. Trousers, for instance: women wear pants because they are practical. (One wonders if this would have made that intrepid feminist, Dolly Bloomer, happy.) It is likely they will go on wearing them as long as they have to do all they have currently to do. Women slop about in shapeless, loose garments because they are comfortable. They wear sandals and sneakers for the same reason. Being lady of the house has ceased to be ritualistic and has become a matter of hard physical activity. All clothes, except possibly the "important" dresses, must be tailored for use, for helpfulness in daily menial work, facility in dressing, ease in caring for. There are no longer maids to serve the mistress. The mistress does her own chores. In the pursuit of social freedom and the mitigation of household drudgery, she has abandoned the crippling liveries that proclaimed her, and indeed rendered her, "the weaker sex." She will not be laced and pressed and stifled. But if she is a healthier woman than her grandmother, if her body, trained by sport and clothed in lighter and freer garments, serves her better and longer, she has forfeited some of her historic charm. Fragility is no longer a permissible allure—nor is incom-

petence; today's wife works. Fainting has gone out of style as walking has come in. The average housewife and mother walks daily at least five miles, carries all of the food supplies, and performs (with mechanical help) the job of five servants and a nurse. No wonder her feet have spread. No wonder she has lost her tiny waist. No wonder she has less patience with the physical distortions that used to be considered aphrodisiacal. She spends all her efforts on head and hair, and goes mad in ecstasies of erotic fancy from the neck up. Below the neck she keeps a worker's body, and she keeps it in prime order. She clothes it in the working uniform of the coolie.

But the changes tempt her to try bolder freedoms. There is more than practicality in the assumption of boys' pants for all but ceremonial occasions. Does she indeed long to equate herself with her sons as well as her daughters? In several ways I think she does, and the fact that so many analysts have to reassure female patients about the essential value and happiness of womanhood would support this view. For thousands of years women have observed that womanhood was neither valuable nor happy in the eyes of the community, but in the struggle for equal status the girls would appear to be going to extremes.

They do not, however, go to the extremes our fashion magazines suggest. I have yet to observe young matrons lying around campus, hearth, or salon in gynecological postures. They may be sloppy and comfortable when

they are alone, but in coed classes they tend to sit up and keep their knees off the back of the chairs. And it seems unlikely that Mama, unless blind drunk, would lie on the floor at a cocktail party, or welcome her guests spraddled like Anthony Quinn facing up to the cattle rustlers. It just wouldn't be becoming, no matter what eye make-up she wears.

She does most certainly, however, wear pants. Indeed she borrows all of Buster's outfits, including his space-man, commando, outlaw, cowboy, and sheriff suits, just as little sister does. (Boys and girls today, and even Mama, too, appear to have similar dreams.) And there are whole businesses geared to supply them with the accoutrements of the fantasy life.

Formerly, children did not have to go so far afield for inspiration. I recently saw paper dolls of the 1880's, men dolls as well as women. The alternate suits provided for the Papa doll were a professor's cap and gown, bishop's robes, and full dress Army and naval uniform. There was one business or everyday suit, in this case a Prince Albert cutaway. I venture to say there is not in existence currently a paper doll's wardrobe that includes bishop's robes.

The savage child wears the feathers and paints of a warrior because war is his father's business; he acquires his weapons, his cicatrices, and his plumes formally under Daddy's instruction. Does the son of a Madison Avenue executive sob and pine for a gray flannel suit and a brief

case? No. He is given the suit young and he wears it for all family ceremonies, but for choice he dresses more frequently as an astronaut.

The desire to wear romantic masquerade in everyday life, to dress more romantically, more alluringly, than Papa, began in the nineteenth century with the emergence of big business and the disappearance of the frontier. Papa may have been doing staggering things with ticker tape, but he did not do them publicly and in special robes. To a child's mind, as to that of an aborigine, appearance matters—and just in the way that direct physical courage is more appealing than moral valor or skill or wisdom, magic is always more impressive than training or conduct. Would it be possible for a child today to dress up as a Selma marcher, we wonder? Or a research chemist? This is unlikely. The most popular physical adventurers now seem to be jerking about in interplanetary space, and, while very few boys have fathers who do this, they all hasten to wear the hats.

The truth is that boys previously wished to look like their fathers. Now they wish not to. Neatness is considered the mark of a responsible adult male, but the boys make a cult of the unkempt. It is the custom for most fathers to clip their hair; the lads wear locks. Heads of families are sober in garment and disdain fancy ornamentation; the boys are ostentatious and embrace decoration, recognizing no differentiation between male and female ornament except as to facial make-up. The boys

have not yet gone so far as to accept any of the classic female distortions—pointed shoes, high heels, and corsets —but they have not accepted any of the classic male distortions either: scarring, cicatricing, or tattooing. Our young warriors have not, in fact, gone through any accepted initiation rites. Their badges of manhood have been pre-empted at random with the aim only of being contrary. They follow youth's historic tradition of being as noisily difficult and as noticeable as possible. But this revolt is remarkable in that it cuts across all classes. Little sister likes attention too, and she tags along. What is important to know is that she is no longer rebuked—she can do or wear almost anything she likes.

We have before us, then, this curious cycle: Mama imitates her daughter, who imitates big brother, who is revolting against Papa in the strongest form he can find to express disapproval; namely, un-masculinity as it is laid down by tradition. He goes fancy and feminine; i. e., toward Mama. In fact, the young men now seem to dress as young women masquerading as boys.

Exaggerations in the differentiation of sex, as well as confusions—transferences of sexual characteristics, for example—are fever symptoms of social reconstruction. Obviously, our civilization is roiling up from the bottom; this is reflected in relations between the sexes, not to mention the relation of parent to child, of citizen to government, class to class, and culture to culture.

Similar periods in the past can be charted by a cyclical pattern in dress: wild extravagance, followed by an abrupt return to romanticism—then revolution or war. The preparation for overt violence always seems to be heralded by an evocation of idealism, romance, and noble sexual characterization. These manifestations are not causal—they are symptomatic only—but they are apparent and recurring.

It is ironic that we in our present masquerades might well dread the moment when the boys suddenly, without seeming adequate motivation, want to look virile again— like father; and when the girls put on provocative and lovely robes—like father's true love. Today, however, the element of time has been withdrawn, and the historic sequence may not be given the opportunity of achieving itself. Symptoms now lag behind instantaneous fact; Armageddon may on the instant arrive without its customary sartorial prelude. Indeed, we may all die without having anything suitable to wear.

Agnes de Mille won the 1966 Capezio Dance Award for her achievements as "dancer, choreographer, writer, and crusader." In the third of these roles she is the author of Dance to the Piper, And Promenade Home (*both autobiographical*), To a Young Dancer, The Book of the Dance.

Maria Theresa never took a lover, never had anyone shot, countered her husband's dalliance by setting up "chastity police," and managed her difficult realm like a well-run household

MOTHER
to the
FATHERLAND

By DOROTHY McGUIGAN

The great golden palace of Schönbrunn was Maria Theresa's favorite residence. This view of the main courtyard was painted by Bernardo Bellotto

As heiress to the Habsburg domains, Maria Theresa was Archduchess of Austria, Queen of Hungary and Bohemia, Statthalter of the Netherlands, and Duchess of Milan. To these titles she later added that of empress, when her husband was elected to the rather empty honors of the Holy Roman Empire. Since she was abler and more responsible than he, there was never any doubt as to who was the real ruler. In her piety, her devotion to her husband, and her tireless matchmaking she recalls that later matriarch, Queen Victoria, more than she does her own contemporary, Catherine the Great. But she shares with the latter the distinction of being one of the two most formidable women of the eighteenth century.

The icy wind that blew across central Europe the autumn of 1740, freezing the vines and ruining the wine crop, chilling and killing the Emperor Charles VI, presaged a winter long remembered in Austria; it was the bitterest of Maria Theresa's life.

She was twenty-three years old and pregnant with her fourth child when her father lay on his deathbed. Her physicians would not allow her to bid him good-bye; in the last hours of his life, the dying emperor turned in the direction of his daughter's room and raised his arms in a gesture of benediction.

She needed that blessing.

In spite of all that her father had done to buy the right

Maria Theresa, her husband Franz, and eleven of their thirteen surviving children were painted on a balcony at Schönbrunn by Martin van Meytens, one of several court painters who had a hard time keeping up with the fast-growing family (Maria Theresa bore sixteen children in twenty years). The matrimonially unlucky Crown Prince, Joseph, is standing to the left of his mother.

of succession to the Habsburg domains for her, his death was the signal to loose a great Europe-wide succession war. Frederick of Prussia—not yet Great—grabbed Silesia before the young and inexperienced queen had so much as put on her crown; she would hate him all her life for it. In her own country everything was at sixes and sevens. Provoked by cold and misery, people rioted in Vienna in the month after Charles's death. There was no standing army to defend the country and no money to raise one. Morale was at low ebb. Her own ministers—old, old men, all but one in their seventies—hadn't the slightest faith in the ability of a young and pretty woman to rule anything. The English ambassador, Robinson, wrote home: " 'Oh,' cryed the Chancellor to me, 'were she but a man with the very same endowments she has!' "

In the deep anxieties of that winter, Maria Theresa wrote her mother-in-law, the Dowager Duchess of Lorraine, that she did not know where to go to await in peace the birth of her child. Terrible personal anguish beset her. Only the previous June her eldest child, a bright pretty little girl of three, had died within hours, stricken by a mysterious ailment. Now, again within the space of a few hours, her youngest child sickened and died. It must have seemed that her whole safe and familiar world was being torn to shreds, and she herself helpless to stop it.

The crown of the Holy Roman Empire passed out of the hands of the Habsburgs, for only the second time in centuries. No woman could wear that crown; Maria Theresa had wanted desperately to see it bestowed on her husband, Franz of Lorraine. Once again France intervened to support the rival candidate. The Elector of Bavaria was chosen instead.

One by one all the signatories to those treaties her father had bought so dearly now abandoned her. The Prussians defeated the Austrian forces at Mollwitz, in Silesia. France and Bavaria prepared to carve up the Habsburg Empire. In Paris, Cardinal Fleury announced to the world, "There is no more House of Austria!"

But they counted without the remarkable courage and energy of Maria Theresa: a born worker, she was in her cabinet or at the council table from daybreak until late at night, conferring, planning, dictating, maneuvering, almost literally holding together with sheer strength of will the breaking package.

In March she was in childbed. Suddenly her whole country took on fresh hope: a boy was born, the first male in the family in a quarter of a century, and not a mere boy baby but a hulking great Hercules of a child, who was said to have weighed sixteen pounds at birth.

In June of 1741 Maria Theresa was crowned Queen of Hungary and rode up the Coronation Mount at Pressburg on a white charger, wearing the tattered mantle of Saint Stephen, to defy with her saber the four corners of the earth.

That summer a Bavarian army threatened to invade Austria, with a French army on the way to join it. Maria Theresa had virtually no army to defend her country. She called the Hungarian Diet to Pressburg and pled her cause in person before the Magnates, men who bore bitter resentment against the Habsburgs for a century of harsh treatment since the Thirty Years' War. Still in deep mourning for her father, the Queen's dark gown set off admirably her fair skin and pretty shoulders. Under the crown of Saint Stephen her blonde hair fell in curls to her shoulders.

At the end of her moving plea for help, when she burst into very real tears, the Magnates could no longer contain themselves and leapt to their feet, drawing their sabers and crying, "Our life and blood for Your Majesty!" More important, they voted her six regiments.

The Bavarians were driven out of her lands. The crown of the Holy Roman Empire went to Maria Theresa's husband, Franz, and eventually the French made peace.

She embarked then on the two great themes of her reign: the unification of her multilingual lands—the theme, in fact, of all Habsburg history—and the achievement of that revolution in European diplomacy, the Habsburg-French alliance.

The palace nurseries were simply bursting with children. There were sixteen in all. During the first half of her reign, when Maria Theresa was plunged into a long series of wars and difficult diplomatic moves, when she had to cope with the reorganization of her army and finances, and the administering of the most complex realm in all Europe, she was always either pregnant or nursing a child.

It was maddening that her archenemy, Frederick of Prussia, could ride at the head of his troops and move them about with lightning swiftness, while she had to direct things from home. "No one," she declared once, thinking of her dawdling Austrian generals, "would have prevented me from joining my armies myself, had I not continuously been pregnant." And yet she was a thoroughly feminine woman who believed that a woman's place was by the cradle and at her husband's side, as she told her own daughters time and again; *she* happened to

This lead statue by Franz Xavier Messerschmidt commemorates Maria Theresa's coronation in 1741 as Queen of Hungary ("Queen" to everyone else; to the proud Magyars, unable to accept the idea of a female sovereign, she was "our Mistress and King"). Maria Theresa's success in winning over the Hungarians, who had no enthusiasm for Habsburg rule, was one of her greatest achievements. She paid for it, however, with concessions that gave Hungary an increasingly independent role in the Habsburg monarchy—which, in our time, broke down under the strain.

OSTERREICHISCHE GALERIE, VIENNA

Until she went into permanent mourning for her husband in 1765, Maria Theresa thoroughly enjoyed the brilliant court life of which she was the center—whether it took the form of some glittering spectacle like a ladies' tournament in the Winter Riding School of the Hofburg (above), or of a private recital by the Mozart family at Schönbrunn (below).

rule because it was the will of God and her duty.

They were feminine talents that she brought to her queenship: tact, compassion, human understanding. She had an eye for the right person in the right job; unlike her father and grandfather, she was quick to recognize and reward talent. The old, old men disappeared from her council table. For chancellor she got the shrewdest statesman in continental Europe, Count Wenzel Kaunitz; a clever Silesian, Count Haugwitz, handled army reform; a Bohemian, Count Chotek, reorganized taxation. She never found a general to match the great Prince Eugene, who had died three months after her wedding, but she made out with the best she could get—a Scotsman, Laudon, and an Irishman, Lacy. She herself saw that her soldiers were properly fed, clothed, blanketed. Her ministers and generals gave her unswerving loyalty; she was like one of those shrewd, capable Austrian housewives whose servants stay with them a lifetime.

She hadn't a shred of intellectual brilliance; the Enlightenment was a fearful bogy on which she firmly shut her country's door. But she had three things even more important in a ruler: sound judgment, a generous spirit, and an enormous store of physical and spiritual stamina. She worked indefatigably; she danced tirelessly; she simply could not bear to waste time. She would drive very fast out of the city to her summer palace of Schönbrunn, the windows of her carriage flung open, like the windows of her apartment, winter and summer, so that her ladies in waiting shivered and her hair blew about her face. She would roll through the great gates between the slender obelisks, grandly tossing out a handful of gold pieces to her guards, and drive across the courtyards that bustled with carriages, market women, dragoons on guard, barefoot friars. Jumping down lightly at the great front door, she would hurry inside and, in a few minutes, be bent over her desk, writing those interminable memorandums, letters to ambassadors, instructions to her children's tutors—all dashed off in a rapid scrawl with the most perfunctory attention to spelling and grammar.

Though her chamberlain, Count Silva-Tarouca, would reprimand her delicately for her inattention to dress, she was a handsome woman and a regal one, and she understood perfectly how to create an imperial image. She could make a splendid appearance in the throne room, magnificently gowned, with the gift her husband had brought from the treasures of his lost Lorraine, a huge diamond called "the Florentine," sparkling on her forehead; or, equally, in the carrousel coach, shaped like an open seashell and filled with fresh flowers, in which she rode through the streets of Vienna like a youthful Venus Anadyomene. But as long as her husband lived she gave the impression of beauty, in itself a considerable talent.

Perhaps what most captivated her admirers was her warmth and naturalness, and her immense capacity for enjoying herself: at gala evenings in the palace, on horseback in the Vienna Woods with her husband at her side, or in that wonderful canopied bed in the Hofburg, where her solemn duty to the Empire coincided so perfectly with her own inclinations. It is clear from contemporary accounts that she laughed a great deal. Until 1765 she masked and danced and played jokes during *Fasching*, the annual carnival season. When her mentor, Count Silva-Tarouca, thought she was enjoying it too much and sent her an earnest reminder of her duties as a monarch, she returned the memo with a marginal comment, "Remind me again when Lent begins."

Goethe has a description of her standing on a balcony in Frankfurt as her husband's coronation procession emerged from the church in 1745; when Franz raised his hands and gestured up to show her the old red-and-gold gloves, the orb and scepter, she had laughed and clapped her hands with delight, as she had once long ago as a little girl when she had first seen her father in his imperial robes walking past in the Corpus Christi procession.

As for the formal court etiquette that had ruled the Hofburg for so long, Maria Theresa brushed it away with a wave of her fan and a laugh of high good humor. Her father and her grandfather, both shy men who could not bear the world jostling at their elbows, used etiquette to keep the crowd at a distance. Maria Theresa neither needed nor wanted it. She made it perfectly easy for her subjects to see her. At her audiences each morning at ten, anyone who wished might speak quite freely, even whisper in her ear on a very private matter.

When the Mozart family made their first appearance in Vienna, Maria Theresa had them out to Schönbrunn where the two children, little Wolfgang and his sister, performed for the imperial family, and as Leopold wrote his wife: ". . . their Majesties received us with such extraordinary graciousness that when I describe it, people will not believe me. Suffice it to say that Wölferl jumped upon the lap of the Empress, put his arms around her neck and kissed her heartily."

And when, later in her reign, her first grandson was born, that precious and terribly important heir to the Habsburg throne, a messenger brought the news to her while she was working late at her desk in the Hofburg. Dropping her papers, she went rushing through the corridors of the palace in negligee and out into the loge of the Court Theatre, where a crowd had gathered to hear an opera. Leaning over the imperial box she called down, "Children! children! My Poldi has a boy! And on my wedding anniversary!" The pit was electrified and burst into thunderous applause.

One of the legends in Austria of Maria Theresa—which, like most apocryphal legends of the great, no doubt contains its kernel of truth—relates that as she walked in the garden of Schönbrunn with her infant son Joseph and his nurse, they came upon a beggarwoman holding a screaming baby to her empty breast. The Empress stopped at once to open her purse; the woman turned away with an angry gesture, saying bitterly that a gold piece would not quiet her hungry babe. Thereupon the Empress picked up the squalling child and put it to her own ample breast.

There had never been a doubt that her marriage, for all its political efficacy, was one of true love. When she was only twenty-four and had been married only half a dozen years, Maria Theresa ordered her tomb to be built in the Kapuzinerkirche. On the lid of that necrophilic masterpiece the imperial couple recline gracefully, as they might have flung themselves down on a flowery hillside at Schönbrunn, youthful, ardent, about to make love. It is not at all the usual royal tomb portrait. The Empress's low-cut court gown displays her handsome shoulders and breast, and, as a contemporary English visitor wrote home delicately, "The posture of the Emperor . . . it must be owned is a little equivocal." While an angel holds a wreath above their heads, they gaze into one another's eyes for all eternity. The Empress must have said, "I will have it so, in marble, and forever."

The truth was that her husband's attention was straying.

Franz of Lorraine was by all accounts a delightful man and a kind one, good-looking, cultivated, charming. He hunted well, danced with grace, made love beautifully—he had, after all, learned at the court of France. His wife had got him crowned Holy Roman Emperor, that one crown that no woman could wear, and had hoped he would prove a military, or at least a diplomatic, genius. Franz was neither. The Empress stopped consulting him about matters of war and state; in the end he had nothing at all to do except to fulfill his functions as her husband.

That voluptuous shared bedroom in the Hofburg must finally have become irksome. For years his wife was nearly always pregnant. She kept, besides, atrocious hours —rising at four in summer, at five in winter, working energetically through the day, going to bed at a decent hour so that she might rise again and work at dawn.

Before long gossip got about that the Emperor Franz was flirting, that there were private, very amusing supper parties with a pretty dancer. The Prussian ambassador wrote home with undisguised malice that the Empress wished to keep a *ménage bourgeois*, but that the Emperor was not being entirely co-operative.

It was not a delicate age and morals in Vienna were far from tidy. Comedy both on stage and off was apt to be coarser and bawdier than either in England or in France. Such an event as the birth of an heir to the throne could be greeted with exceedingly gross public utterances. Some of Mozart's songs, written for the amusement of his friends in merry evenings at home, are, like the scatological letters to his little cousin in Augsburg, scarcely printable, but they are not at all out of keeping with the age and place.

Perhaps her husband's peccadilloes provoked the Empress's innate puritanism into action. Her decision was on a typically imperial scale: she would simply abolish vice throughout her

realm. She was perfectly sure she could rule morals as efficiently as she handled taxation and supplies for the army. And so in 1747 she proceeded to set up a Chastity Commission, its purpose simply to enforce virtue in public and private.

Chastity police were posted at theatres and ballrooms. They patrolled the streets with orders to arrest girls found walking alone. At the Austrian borders they ransacked the luggage of travelers and even went through diplomatic mailbags to extract naughty books—or the works of the French philosophers.

Prostitutes were transported to southern Hungary, where a possibly unique village was said to have been populated almost entirely with the banished ladies. Streetwalkers learned quickly to avoid arrest by walking demurely, head down, ostentatiously fingering a rosary.

Chastity police followed up reports brought by jealous wives and counterreports by jealous husbands. Easygoing Vienna howled—first with dismay, then with amusement. A crowd of fast young men about town organized an intriguing secret society called the Fig Leaf Brotherhood, with the avowed purpose of thwarting the chastity commissioners. Their feminine equivalent, the Order of Free Ladies, met with them for gay parties, wearing, gossip reported, chiefly masks and pseudonyms. Once, when police raided a party of Fig Leaf Brothers, the offenders were sentenced to be shackled at the city gates to beg their food and drink from passersby. But none of them had to beg, for citizens flocked to the gates bringing delicacies and sympathy.

Casanova visited Vienna just then with a mistress on whom he had bestowed the gratuitous title of countess.

The day after their arrival they were surprised at breakfast by a visit from the chastity police, and when Casanova admitted that he was a bachelor, he was forced to move immediately into separate quarters. Ruefully, he wrote that "there was plenty of money and plenty of luxury in Vienna, but the bigotry of

CONTINUED ON PAGE 110

Maria Theresa's principal diplomatic weapon was the marriage contract—and with her numerous offspring she had ample opportunity to exercise it. Only one child, "Mimi," had her own way, and her marriage to Albert of Saxony was the only happy one. The porcelain group at left commemorates the betrothal, the painting opposite the wedding feast.

CARL AUENBA...
1773

1ᵉʳ Janvier 1888.

Youssouf Bey

The artist in diplomatic mufti

THE WORLD OF

An album of satiric

by a talented Ottoman diplom

the internatio

Control of Constantinople, Napoleon once declared, "means the empire of the world." He was simply confirming a political judgment shared by every major power in Europe: that land-locked Russia, the principal obstacle to the expansion of the other European powers, would remain harmless as long as possession of the Straits separating the two continents and linking the Black Sea with the Mediterranean eluded its grasp. The great gate city of Constantinople, as the key to both these objectives, thus became a focal point of all the complex treaty making that occupied the West from the Congress of Vienna in 1815 to the outbreak of World War I, a century later.

The European community could not have chosen a more fascinating site to act out the last stages of territorial expansion. Constantinople's marvelous setting on the Bosporus, its sprawling, pungent bazaars, the opulence of its many palaces, the contrasts of its European and Asian quarters laced together by the languid shuttle of caïques, were Turkish delights to Westerners who had been educated to admire order and productivity as the ultimate attainments of civilization.

Yet, Istanbul, as the Turks preferred to call their capital, was still the center of a backward state, enlivened under the reign of Abdul Hamid (1876–1909) by all the worst features of despotism and intrigue. Its people were a fractious mixture of religious and racial groups, running from tribal nomads to the most cosmopolitan bureaucrats. The scientific, technological, and social revolutions that had made Progress the rallying cry in the Occident had

barely begun to trouble the Ottoman mind, and such reforms as were achieved failed to change long-held European judgments. "Pretentious and superb, ignorant and deceitful, dirty and disordered; still submerged in the medieval superstitions . . . where good is bad, and reason marches arm and arm with nonsense . . . the city of the Ottoman emperors presents all in all the most strange and incomprehensible character," said one baffled observer. To another, Istanbul was simply *"la ville de méprise mutuel."*

Unfortunately, these highly prejudiced accounts have played a disproportionate role in our ideas of the city and its people since few accounts by the Turkish hosts reached Western readers. Then, too, Turks did not have the same opportunities to form impressions of others, for they rarely traveled outside the empire; foreign trade had never been a significant part of Ottoman expansion, and the "Sublime Porte," as the government was known, did not establish legations in other major capitals until the end of the eighteenth century, more than two centuries after European representatives had begun to settle in Constantinople.

By the rarest good fortune, a brilliant insight into the attitudes of one member of the educated class toward these foreigners has recently come to light. In the 1880's and 1890's, when the international role that had been forced on Istanbul was at its dramatic peak, Youssouf Bey Franco, a loyal Ottoman participant in and observer of the goings-on, compiled an album of extraordinary drawings in which he caricatured with unsparing wit

YOUSSOUF BEY

...awings, only recently discovered,

...ovides an intimate glimpse of

...bal that dismembered "the sick man of Europe"

By WENDY BUEHR

Conférence de Constantinople

Novembre 1885

As a junior member of the foreign service, Youssouf Bey (at right in the palace interior above, with his back to us) had ample opportunity to observe conference diplomacy at work. What he saw was a rich mixture of politics and poker, a gentlemanly game in which, by prearrangement, the Ottoman Empire was to be systematically relieved of all its non-Turkish holdings. The players at this session are, in clockwise order after the Sultan's befezzed envoys at left, the ministers of Britain, Russia, Germany, France, Austria-Hungary, Italy.

Au pays des roupies.

During his influential career, Lord Dufferin (right) represented the British Empire in almost every capital of the civilized world, including a brief period in Istanbul from 1881 to 1882. Described by one member of the European community as "a grand seigneur to the tips of his fingernails," Dufferin made a similarly imperious impression on Youssouf Bey, whose memories of the man are recorded in this caricature made several years after the ambassador had gone on to become viceroy of India. Britain's consuming interest in all its colonies and the sea routes that connected them determined in large part its policy toward the Sultan's territories. Sir Henry Drummond Wolff (opposite, shown on the banks of the Nile) was twice sent to Constantinople to reassure the Turks after the British armies had occupied Ottoman Egypt and Suez in 1882. The envoy's foot planted firmly on an agreement for the eventual return of Egypt indicates the artist's view of the matter.

virtually every significant personage on the local scene —including himself. Despite his obvious sympathy with the Sultan's cause, the delightful and incisive essays shown on these pages have apparently never been reproduced before.

Not a great deal is known about the life of this talented artist. At the time that Youssouf Bey painted these caricatures he was just beginning in his government's foreign service, a career that would give him official and social entree into the European colony. In the conference scene shown on page 25, he is a member of the secretariat; he eventually rose to the top of his profession, becoming before World War I, governor of the tiny but autonomous state of Lebanon and foreign minister of the dwindling empire. The many relatives portrayed in the album suggest that he came from a family of considerable culture and broad connections in public life. He was a native of Aleppo in northern Syria; we know, too, that like many men in the Moslem foreign office, he was a Chris-

tian—a Greek Catholic—which was considered an advantage in dealing with Europeans; his picture titles tell us that he was fluent in French, the language of diplomacy. Most impressive, however, is his achievement as an artist, equal in wit and skill to the great Max Beerbohm, whose work would not appear for another decade or two. With no tradition of caricature in the East to guide him, and only limited exposure to Greek and French prototypes, Youssouf Bey emerges as a highly original and talented observer.

To appreciate the irony and the political inferences of the portraits, we must take a brief glance at Turkish history. Constantinople's indomitable role over more than sixteen hundred years of history is largely the result of geography. Straddling the narrow Bosporus, the eastern end of the Straits that connect the Black Sea with the Sea of Marmara and ultimately with the major trade routes of the world, Constantinople held one of the most controversial pieces of real estate in the world. Within

its walls are remnants of the ancient and much contested Greek port of Byzantium, founded in the seventh century B.C., and of the early Christian capital established by Constantine in A.D. 330 and defended by his Byzantine successors for a thousand years. Their magnificent monument, Hagia Sophia, is still a dominant feature of the Istanbul skyline, but clusters of smaller domes and slender minarets* testify to the city's Islamic conversion under the Ottoman sultans after 1453 and the resulting break with European culture. Making Constantinople their seat of government, with a single-minded devotion the Ottomans set about spreading the Faith and, not incidentally, filling the royal treasury to overflowing. Before their military machine finally exhausted itself in the sixteenth century, the empire was more powerful than any state in Europe. Its armies had all but reached Vienna in the West and held secure the land from the Adriatic to the central Caucasus, south to the Arabian Sea, and along the North African coast as far as the frontiers of Morocco. The

* See "The Golden Horn" in HORIZON for Winter, 1966.

grand design began to falter only after the death of Suleiman the Magnificent in 1566. His hereditary successors, branded by one European as "incompetents, degenerates, and misfits," could not in any case combat the sickness that beset the empire.

Turkey's decline was viewed by the major powers—England, France, Germany, Austria, Russia, and Italy—as an opportunity to extend their separate interests and as a threat to the general peace which had been so carefully wrought at the Congress of Vienna following Napoleon's final defeat. The parceling out of the various prizes, held ever more feebly by "the sick man of Europe," must be accomplished with a delicacy that would not upset the balance of forces or revive old rivalries. The Ottoman Empire, if handled wisely, might even assist at its own dismantling.

It was thus that the fraternity of European nations took in as a full member its first non-Christian state, introducing patterns of negotiation that would reach maturity in

the League of Nations. In the end, the Ottoman Empire disappeared; all its non-Turkish provinces in the Balkans became sovereign states and the provinces in Asia and Africa, dependencies of European nations. Only Istanbul and the Anatolian heartland survived to become the modern republic of Turkey.

The succession of multilateral agreements dealing with these transfers included a London convention internationalizing the Straits in 1841; the 1856 Peace of Paris terminating the Crimean War and guaranteeing Ottoman sovereignty; an agreement in 1861 giving Youssouf Bey's Christian Lebanon semi-autonomy under international guarantees; the Congress of Berlin of 1878 rescinding some particularly harsh terms imposed on the Turks by Russia; and an agreement in 1881 between Sultan Abdul Hamid and his European creditors for the repayment of loans. By the 1880's the almost constant attention that such mounting obligations demanded had created in Istanbul the unique conditions of continuous conference diplomacy that prompted these caricatures.

As serious as the discussions were, the European community evidently had more than enough compensation for its troubles. A professor at Robert College in Istanbul

recalled of one envoy: "The position of the British Ambassador at Constantinople is almost Vice-regal, the salary but little less than the President of the United States. An immense Winter Palace in Pera [the European quarter of the city] and one for the summer hardly less sumptuous on the Bosporus, gunboats and dispatch boats, and steam launches, trains of carriages and horses constantly at his disposal, troops of deputy attachés and household servants, and crimson-coated soldiers, and gilt-bedecked canvasses maintained for his convenience and splendor by Great Britain, and a hundred accessories more, of almost knightly rank and state, are outward manifestations of his dignity and grandeur."

The same might have been said of the ministers of the other powers with the exception of the United States, whose ambitions of conquest still lay on its own continent. In the measured words of Samuel Cox, our man in Istanbul in 1885, the envoy's job was "to view calmly the progress of events in the Orient [synonymous with the Ottoman Empire to a provincial American] with a view to seize every demonstration of war as an opportunity for commercial America." As an outsider, Cox had little use for the cavortings of his European counterparts: "The

Transcendant objections to French expansion in North Africa and Russian expansion in the Balkans had forged the Triple Alliance of Austria-Hungary, Germany, and Italy in 1882, represented in this period by the three men at left. These uneasy partners, who after Italy's defection became the Central Powers of World War I, could barely suppress their many conflicts. The principal concern of the portly Baron Calice (far left) was to maintain the Habsburg influence gained in the Balkans when the Congress of Berlin awarded Austria-Hungary the protectorate of Bosnia-Herzgovinia after it had been won by Russia in its 1878 war with the Sultan. Germany, having assiduously avoided Middle East entanglements under Bismarck, began in the 1880's to insinuate itself in Ottoman politics through technical and economic missions. Joseph von Radowitz (center), the intractable Prussian ambassador in Constantinople, is pictured with a toy soldier, a reference to the military advisers sent by Germany to modernize the Sultan's army. The spidery Baron Galvagna (near left), sketched against the Bosporus landscape, briefly seconded Count Corti of Italy; he is dismissed, in a visual pun, as a boot polisher. Russia's neurasthenic Alexandr Nelidov (below) was just beginning his fourteen-year term in Istanbul when Youssouf Bey bundled him into this imaginary troika. As the principal opponent to European plans for the neutralization of the Straits, he looks understandably apprehensive.

Foreign dress and foreign culture were much admired by Youssouf Bey's more urbane countrymen. The dapper gentleman at right, strictly Bond Street from his stiff wing collar to his pristine spats, is a high-ranking officer in the Ottoman government, though he might be mistaken for an aging English stage-door johnny. Indeed, European theatre and its trappings were sufficiently admired to bring so luminous a figure as Sarah Bernhardt to the Bosporus capital on at least two of her grand tours. She was sketched below on a visit in 1889 when La Tosca *and* La Dame aux camélias *were on the bill.*

10 Janvier 1889.

principal conversation among the various embassies and their attachés concerns riding parties, lawn tennis, dances, dogs, horses, and flirtations."

Mr. Cox, had he been a more perceptive fellow, would have recognized that international politics is not a game limited to the conference table. In an era when personal diplomacy was an honored tradition, something more substantive than gossip was often exchanged at a garden party, and one imagines that the progress of the day's negotiations might depend on the brilliance of the participants the evening before.

Youssouf Bey's caricatures contain many subtle references to this fact. He also records that the Turkish hosts were, by the 1880's, outwardly as comfortable with Western amenities as the Europeans. Wearing stiff collars and cutaway coats, albeit topped with the traditional red fez, they had begun the transformation that Atatürk made central to his reforms in the 1920's when he proclaimed to his pantalooned countrymen: "A civilized, international dress is worthy and appropriate for our nation, and we will wear it." Ironically, Atatürk's ambition to modernize Turkey would lead him to move the nation's capital to Ankara in the hinterland, far away from Youssouf Bey's Istanbul where so many of the newly adopted Western ways had first been learned.

Interpretation of the Youssouf Bey caricatures is based on material generously provided by J. C. Hurewitz, Professor of Government on the Graduate Faculty of Political Sciences and the Middle East Institute, Columbia University. He is the author of several books, including Diplomacy in the Near and Middle East, *Princeton, 1956.*

No one was guaranteed immunity from Youssouf Bey's acid commentary, not even his peers in the legal office of the Ottoman foreign office (left). He parodies the chief custodians and interpreters of government treaties as a parrot, a duck, and a monkey, and subtitles them "ménagerie consultative" to underscore the point. In mock atonement for these and other unflattering portraits, the cartoonist closes his album with "L'Expiation" (below), in which former victims become his joyful executioners. Only his family, in the foreground, replete with handkerchiefs, appears to find his departure "untimely."

L'EXPIATION

"That blue-eyed darling Nathaniel"

Nathaniel Hawthorne at thirty-six, painted by Charles Osgood

Thus did D. H. Lawrence sourly describe Hawthorne,

adding that the man "knew disagreeable things

in his inner soul." Perhaps. But does it really

matter, if he gave us The Scarlet Letter?

*I*n the middle of 1849, during a summer of torrid heat in Salem, Massachusetts, the contending forces in Hawthorne's life were drawing into battle formation, as for a civil war long in preparation. His mother lay dying in a guest chamber of his "narrow house." He had just lost the job in the customhouse that had been arranged for him by friends in politics. In the politically motivated hearings that terminated his appointment he had been slandered and deceived by pious hypocrites among the Whig opposition.

The financial problems that had marred his courtship and harassed the first seven years of his belated marriage still plagued him, and were proving all the more malignant for having been postponed. Add to the practical pressures the fact that he was a man of New England conscience to whom failure was a matter of shame.

For four years his literary production had been small. No less a critic than Edgar Allan Poe had scolded him for his addiction to allegory, and he himself had said of the stories that made up the bulk of his previous work, "they blossomed in too retired a shade." As shade-scattering as the intellectual contacts of recent years had been, his friendship with Boston transcendentalists had rubbed him raw between the decaying claims of Puritanism and the rude potency of Emersonian optimism.

He was forty-five years old now, and the fame that he had wished for since his college days still flirted just beyond his grasp. It would come too late to offer an appeasement for the knotted emotions that had estranged him from the silent woman dying in his guest room. On one hot evening of that summer he recalled, "I love my mother; but there has been, ever since boyhood, a sort of coldness of intercourse between us, such as is apt to come between persons of strong feelings if they are not managed rightly."

Through the curtains of his mother's sickroom he saw his golden-haired daughter Una at play. He saw in her childish bravura the "untempered light . . . the whole warfare of the mother's spirit . . . perpetuated." "Yes," he heard the little girl say, her voice very clear and distinct, "she's going to die."

When Hawthorne looked back at his mother, he "seemed to see the whole of human existence at once, standing in the dusty midst of it."

This was the summer and these were the furious circumstances in which he began to write *The Scarlet Letter.* In a house full of women that included his two sisters as well as mother, wife, and daughter, he was trying not only to resume and extend his career as a writer but, by a reckless vault of imagination, to reconcile all that was terrible and enchanting in the enigma of a woman's life. While his wife tended the dying woman, he had to work much of the time with his study door open to keep an eye on the children in the yard. Of Una he noted, "There is something that almost frightens me about that child— I know not whether elfish or angelic, but at all events,

supernatural . . . a spirit strangely mingled with good and evil, haunting the house where I dwell." In that summer the task that loomed was simply to seize fear in his bare hands and, while it burned him, to shape of it a novel without precedent in American letters, a unique and brilliant point of light in the constellation of world literature.

What gives *The Scarlet Letter* its bite and terror is not the sexuality from which the action proceeds but the unremitting series of consequences that follow on adultery. Already, as the story opens and Hester Prynne steps from the prison with her bastard child in her arms and a fantastically embroidered gold-and-scarlet A on her breast, the circumstances of lust are in the shadows behind her. Nor will they be shown to the reader by flashback and recollection: " . . . the infant and the shame were real. . . . all else had vanished."

Of course we learn the primary facts of Hester's girlhood in England and of her marriage to the old man of science who now calls himself Roger Chillingworth. And in a burst of defiance and hope just before the last darkness comes on them, she reminds the weak minister who made her pregnant, "What we did had a consecration of its own. We felt it so! We said so to each other!" But whatever consecration of desire there may once have been, and whether the illegitimate union with Arthur Dimmesdale was indeed a truer marriage than her union with the sterile old man, nothing abides except the fact of their transgression.

The virtue of their amorous time is not even denied. It doesn't have to be. It is simply thrown into permanent oblivion by the proliferating falsehoods to which they are now committed. Hawthorne seems to say that the sexual act was, by itself, indifferent. Or, if the romantic mind would rather see it this way, it was a natural good to which nature bade them help themselves. But in the human sphere, he says, such an act is never morally isolated. In its various contexts it disrupts all truths by which the spirit must live.

Hester says, "Truth was the one virtue which I might have held fast." Truth is taken from her by her generous wish to protect Dimmesdale from exposure, and this deception delivers him into the power of the wronged husband. The scarlet letter she is condemned to wear cannot even be a simple emblem of confession and repentance but only the symbol of an eternal remorse.

Dimmesdale envies her the privilege of wearing her badge of shame in public. "Even this much of truth would save me! But, now, it is all falsehood!—all emptiness!— all death!" When, after seven years of inner torment, Dimmesdale makes a public confession from the scaffold of the pillory on which Hester was humiliated before the town, Chillingworth says, "there was . . . no high place nor lowly place, where thou couldst have escaped me—save on this very scaffold!" There the exhausted Dimmesdale falls and dies without hope of a "pure reunion" with Hester. At the last he says, "The law we

By R. V. CASSILL

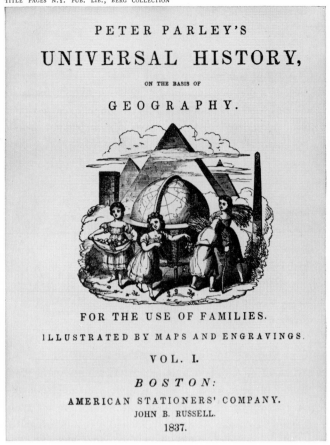

PETER PARLEY'S
UNIVERSAL HISTORY,
ON THE BASIS OF
GEOGRAPHY.

FOR THE USE OF FAMILIES.

ILLUSTRATED BY MAPS AND ENGRAVINGS.

VOL. I.

BOSTON:
AMERICAN STATIONERS' COMPANY.
JOHN B. RUSSELL.
1837.

Under a pseudonym, Hawthorne wrote this schoolboys' history. It sold a million copies, earned him a hundred dollars.

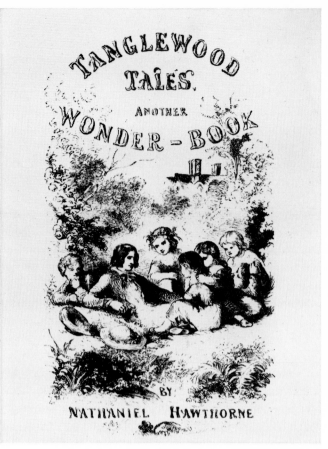

Fifteen years later, success achieved, he turned again to children's literature in a retelling of the classical myths.

broke!—the sin here so awfully revealed!—let these alone be in thy thoughts! I fear! I fear!"

No American novel concludes more sternly or more strictly. This is lamentation, not tragedy, a wail of grief, not a prophecy of renewal. From the "dusty midst" of his life Hawthorne saw a universal field of blackness "relieved only by one ever-glowing point of light *gloomier than the shadow.*"

Here is justification for D. H. Lawrence's comment, "That blue-eyed darling Nathaniel knew disagreeable things in his inner soul. He was careful to send them out in disguise."

Yet for all its gloom and whisper of abominations, *The Scarlet Letter* is among those great tales in which the spectrum of meanings runs unbroken from the clearest daylight into vibrations beyond either vision or rational interpretation. Those who wish to may take it as a historical novel, particularly successful because Hawthorne's predilection for allegory coincides with the tendency of his Puritan protagonists to live their lives allegorically.

It has been taken as a moral sermon, warning against deceit as well as adultery. And, though the term fits awkwardly, it is a novel of protest. Hawthorne was never a liberal, either in the estimation of his transcendental friends or by our lights. He was, nevertheless, appalled by the bigotries of early American life and the deplorable position of colonial women. Hester Prynne is at least nobler than the code by which she is condemned, and we are told, "The angel and apostle of the coming revela-

tion must be a woman indeed . . . lofty, pure, and beautiful; and wise, moreover, not through dusky grief, but the ethereal medium of joy. . . ."

To point out that *The Scarlet Letter* is also a psychological novel obliges one to remark at once that it does not yield very gratefully to Freudian analysis or other currently available methodologies. It waits as patiently as nature for analysts to find the law of its still cryptic utterances—waits perhaps to be read as a deeply disguised self-portrait.

Of nature, Hawthorne says in one of his finest stories, *The Birthmark*, "our great creative Mother, while she amuses us with apparently working in the broadest sunshine, is yet severely careful to keep her own secrets, and, in spite of her pretended openness, shows us nothing but results." The same must be said of the literary artist's imagination.

In every masterpiece we ought to suspect self-portraiture of one type or another. If we cannot yet compose a coherent image of the true man from *The Scarlet Letter*, we can hardly help being tantalized by fragmentary correspondences. For instance, Hawthorne sometimes notes, and more frequently gives active tokens of, the divisions in himself. "A cloudy veil stretches over the abyss of my nature. . . . I have, however, no love of secrecy and darkness." Again and again he reverts to the theme of conflict between head and heart, a conflict whose elements are personified in *The Scarlet Letter* by the two antithetic male characters bound to a single destiny by having shared the body of one woman.

Hawthorne was born to venerate and mistrust women above all other beings. A perfunctory glance at his biography will show how much of his life was lived within what he might call the "female sphere." Was it not from his own deepest experience with marriage—sweet-tempered monogamist though he was—that he glimpsed the echoing doubleness of woman, that he saw the shame inextricably involved in Hester Prynne's nobility?

His other novels, the short stories and sketches, and the unevenly marvelous notebooks he kept throughout his life are foothills around *The Scarlet Letter*. The artist's career and his personal tribulations only revealed their meaning after that book's publication. But to look back, as we, of course, are privileged to do, from beyond this peak is to see that even the circumstances and place of his birth were part of the lucky design culminating in his great novel.

The Salem in which he was born in 1804 was no longer one of the great seaports of the earth. Full of legends and history, it was falling into a dream of old witchcraft and colonial heroism. Here was a town and time for old wives' tales so often repeated that they had become half fabulous. Hawthorne's first years were spent in the poor fringe of great Salem families, so that he would overhear the agitations of power without direct involvement in them. His father, a sea captain and son of sea captains, died on a voyage to Surinam when Hawthorne was four, leaving him to grow up in a house of women.

Rich uncles sent him to Bowdoin College, where he met the friends who were later to shape his life by their political and intellectual support. Longfellow was among his classmates. So was Franklin Pierce, who became the fourteenth President of the United States. Among the more tedious productions to come from Hawthorne's pen was a campaign biography of Pierce, in exchange for which Hawthorne was given the post of American consul in Liverpool after the 1852 election.

By that time, after the success of *The Scarlet Letter*, Hawthorne was one of the most famous American writers. But in the twelve years following his graduation from college in 1825, he was the most invisible. He went back to his mother's house in Salem and, while he began to write steadily and in fact to produce some of his best stories, became an eccentric recluse. There seems to be some exaggeration in the legend that he never went outdoors until after dark and never shared a meal with his mother or sisters. Nevertheless, he was shaping himself into just such a grotesque castaway from life as the ones that people his stories. He must have watched what was happening to himself with horrific fascination, to which we have some clue in this notebook jotting: "A person to be writing a tale, and to find that it shapes itself against his intentions . . . [toward] a catastrophe which he strives in vain to avert. It might shadow forth his own

fate—he having made himself one of the personages." Those who ask where Hawthorne got his sense of personal sin might ponder this, reflecting that a man who binds his soul to any art has made a pact of an uncanny sort. He has chosen something like a permanent alienation from the community of human devotions.

Even when he was publishing several stories each year and those stories had begun to acquire a small, fine reputation, their authorship was kept secret. Queer doings for a young man who had come from college with the hope of seeing his name among those of the "scribbling sons of John Bull"!

It was Elizabeth Peabody, a neighbor and the daughter of a doctor who had treated Hawthorne in childhood, who smoked out his secret and began to introduce him in Salem society as a man of accomplishment. She arranged, too, for his first appointment in the customs service, in Boston. When the Peabody family also moved to that city, it was through them and the circle of intellectuals they cultivated that Hawthorne found a part in the glorious comedy of Brook Farm.

Brook Farm was an experiment in socialist reformation established in 1841 on two hundred acres of land eight miles west of Boston. The project was so small in scale, except for the reputations and character of the personalities involved in it, so poor in resources and deficient in planning, that only the most incontinent of dreamers could have expected its example to change the social currents of the century. Hawthorne was never so impractical as to think it might. Furthermore, he was enough of a conservative to doubt the worth of most social reforms even if they should take hold. But there, in the spring of 1841, we find him investing a thousand dollars for two shares in Utopia and riding out of Boston through a snowstorm to begin work as a farmer.

The move was less a repudiation of existing society than a wild gamble at finding a way into it through the back door. He hoped to find at Brook Farm a living that would permit him to marry. Now approaching forty, he was anxiously in love with Elizabeth Peabody's sister Sophia. Since Elizabeth had shooed him out of his recluse study he had tried his hand at editing as well as serving the customhouse. Neither occupation supplemented his tiny writing income enough to give him confidence that he could sustain a family.

At Brook Farm he predictably caught a cold (or perhaps pneumonia) before he did anything else at all. Recovered, he was put to work on one of the hugest manure piles in the literature of American farming. This and the other hand-hardening chores that were his communal lot produced no more enlightenment than the opinion that "a man's soul may be buried and perish under a dungheap or in a furrow of the field, just as well as under a pile of money." This is hardly one of the weightier rebuttals of romantic sentimentality.

But Brook Farm gave him something, after all. Although his hopes of settling Sophia near its sweetly chattering stream went glimmering from the moment of his first sneeze in the farmhouse parlor, he got his second-best novel, *The Blithedale Romance*, from his observations there.

He was ten years away from Brook Farm before he wrote the book. By then the success of *The Scarlet Letter* had justified his habit of looking at people out of the corner of his eye, of taking his nature walks by moonlight, of personifying abstractions instead of rendering persons, and of converting impressions of lively Yankee contemporaries into "strange portraits of something sad, terrific." The dark half of his genius was vindicated.

All the while he had something else going. Just as there was an extraordinarily sharp distinction between night-self and day-self in the man, there are really two kinds of novelist signing themselves Nathaniel Hawthorne. "Moonlight is sculpture," he wrote in his notebook. "Sunlight is painting." *The Blithedale Romance* is, mostly, a painting in sunlight to complement the sculpture of the earlier and greater novel.

Secondary though it is in most of his fiction, his skill as "painter" shows its growth in his notebooks and the travel essays of *Our Old Home* (1863)—works whose literary value is probably equal to most of the novels and tales. They are the notes of a clear-eyed New Englander alert to the human values, the color and variety, of the people he met in offices, in taverns, at country fairs, and on the mountain roads of his own country or in the slums and offices of Liverpool during his consulship there.

In his notebooks he reports the dialogue of his children, as when his son Julian said "When I grow up I shall be two men," or "Look, papa, there's a bunch of fire." The speech is supple as life compared to the often wooden exchanges in the novels and tales—dialogue, we have to concede, was not the strong point of Hawthorne's art.

The prose of the notebooks never has the gimcrack grandiloquence that stiffens some of the fiction. The swarming notes for the stories—some of them quickly identifiable as the germs of works later completed and published, some of the best never developed—have an epigrammatic precision that we long for in vain amid the tedious laboring and incredibly obtuse repetitions in a couple of the novels.

The legless beggar who haunted Hawthorne's walks in Liverpool (mentioned in an altogether excellent sketch called "Outside Glimpses of English Poverty") is more ominous in his daylight credibility than the goblin figure of the artist's model in *The Marble Faun*.

"There is a fellow hereabout who refuses to pay six dollars for the coffin in which his wife was buried. She died about six months since, and I believe he is already engaged to another. He is young and rather comely, but has not a straightforward look." In such a self-contained fragment from the notebooks a good ear catches the accent of writers we usually consider far removed from

the modes of Nathaniel Hawthorne—Jane Austen, perhaps, or Hardy, or even Chekhov, whose notebooks more often give the same tone as Hawthorne's than a comparison of their fiction could possibly suggest. And elsewhere in the pieces of direct observation and selective reportage one can be convinced that this author was born to write in the manner of Dickens and Balzac.

In *The Blithedale Romance* he did. There are gothic furbelows attached to this novel, also—spook stuff and mystifications to gratify a taste we have long since lost. Yet strip these romantic tatters away and what remains is not only a keen dissection of the Brook Farm idealists, but—in more human and pathetic terms this time—another profound representation of the sexual enigma that lies at the core of *The Scarlet Letter*.

It is said, and usually said with a timidity proper to such identifications, that the character Zenobia in *The Blithedale Romance* is modeled on Margaret Fuller, one of the more ornate transcendentalists and no doubt a real handful during her visits to Brook Farm. As portrait, Zenobia does poor justice to the headlong, gallant, wasteful woman who was the real Margaret Fuller. But in her own right, within the confines of the novel, Zenobia is powerfully realized. Her infatuation with the windbag reformer Hollingsworth is a disturbing comment on the vulnerability of all superior women. The scene in which Hollingsworth fishes for her drowned body with a pole taken from the well is as moving and solemn, as humanly revealing and dramatically effective, as anything in the American novel.

Put this scene beside the great stage effects of *The Scarlet Letter* if you wish to conjecture which side of Hawthorne's genius was potentially the greater. You may conclude that he could have been as eminent in realism as he was in symbolism and allegory.

Hawthorne lost the thousand dollars he invested in Brook Farm without solving any of the problems that had delayed his marriage. So he married Sophia Peabody anyway. He married her while the dust from the collapse of his expectations was still rising in clouds around him.

He married her and they lived triumphantly ever after. At least this is the way the story of our illustrious couple goes, and it must be true or else they would not be illustrious. Of course there were anguishes and scrapes to come. During the crisis period in which *The Scarlet Letter* was written, Sophia believed that Hawthorne was suffering from "brain fever." And one who has never gone into the abyss of his own nature and come back with an emblem of shame and glory—that is, a true work of art—to show the world, need not envy the artist his role.

But the Hawthornes' marriage was a remarkably successful mating. The years of its endurance were altogether gracious enough to dim out of the world's memory the years of Hawthorne's rebellious, half-mad seclusion. It changed the tone of his living sufficiently to permit Henry James to speak of Hawthorne's *whole* life as an "unagitated fortune." All's well that ends in a marriage like Hawthorne's to Sophia, for it was his marriage to a world that he could finally trust.

Sophia had been half an invalid when he met her, somewhat in the style of Elizabeth Barrett Browning. She was given to headaches and periods of "weakness" that had kept her almost as much of a recluse as her husband-to-be. Her health was not instantaneously restored by marriage. Although it greatly improved, it remained uneven through her life. She could be, nevertheless, an energetic traveler, a lively mother to their three children, an eager and adoring echo of her husband in the "lovely strophe and antistrophe" of their permanent dialogue. They even collaborated on a journal of their first months of happiness together.

Their married life began in the Old Manse at Concord. From its windows Hawthorne looked out at the bridge where the battle of Concord began. He fished, bathed, and boated in the Concord River behind the house. He also carried water from the river for Sophia's bath. On the summery days of their honeymoon they lay on a carpet of dried pine needles in the gloom of shade around their house. "There was no wind & the stillness was profound," Sophia wrote. "There seemed no movement in the world but that of our pulses."

Emerson, who lived half a mile away, came to see them. So did Ellery Channing and Thoreau. After Thoreau had been to dinner with them, Hawthorne noted, "He is as ugly as sin, long-nosed, queer-mouthed. . . . But his ugliness is of an honest and agreeable fashion, and becomes him much better than beauty. . . . Nature, in return for his love, seems to adopt him as her especial child, and shows him secrets which few others are allowed to witness."

When Hawthorne, waking at least momentarily from the first enchantment of marriage, spoke worriedly to Emerson about his debts, Emerson unhelpfully pointed out that many others of their acquaintance were in deeper than he. Finally, the publication of *The Scarlet Letter* in the spring of 1850 lightened the financial pressure. That August the Hawthornes took a little red house at Lenox in the Berkshires, moving now, as they would henceforward, in a society heavily salted with writers and artists. In Lenox, James Russell Lowell and Oliver Wendell Holmes came to visit them. Herman Melville lived nearby. His friendship with Hawthorne had begun some years before in their admiration for each other's work. It now became an intense companionship of literary talk, quiet boozing, and speculation on the immortal soul.

They had company there in the mountains, but Hawthorne's taste for society was growing remarkably. When he had finished *The House of the Seven Gables*, he chose to return to a more populous place. During the winter of

The Old Manse in Concord, built by Emerson's grandfather, was rented to Hawthorne after his marriage to Sophia Peabody in 1842. The inscriptions above and below, scratched on a window pane with a diamond, recall this happy time.

1851–52 he moved his family—now including the three children—to West Newton, the town near Boston where he wrote *The Blithedale Romance*. In the spring of 1852 he bought Bronson Alcott's house in Concord, romantically christened it "The Wayside," and meant to make it the home of his declining years.

The intent did not materialize. This man whose roots penetrated so deeply into the past of Salem never really settled elsewhere after he had severed them. In 1853 he and his family sailed for Liverpool, where the United States consulship awaited him. The four years he spent there, outwardly serene, proved another curious lurch in the destiny of the artist. He was probably a much better than average consul. A conscientious man with a novelist's sympathy and insight into the problems of fellow citizens abroad would naturally be. He made enough money in four years to show why a consulship was then such a desirable political prize. Yet, at the height of his powers, with a sounder preparation than any American contemporary for fictional tasks still uncompleted, he wrote no fiction to speak of. Like many American writers who followed him, he had come up to a plateau of eminence that was just too comfortable to dive from. What happy family man and respected public servant could voluntarily turn back from that sunlit height into the haunted mire from which his art had successfully raised him?

In the years left to him, however, he proved that he was not through as a writer. In Italy, where he took his family for a protracted stay after his consulship terminated, he started to shape the outlines for the most ambitious of his novels, *The Marble Faun*. It was to be nothing less than the re-created legend of man's fall, a kind of novelistic *Paradise Lost* where pagan myths were mingled with Christian doctrine and dressed in the circumstances of nineteenth-century Roman life.

The "faun" Donatello was to represent the legendary Adam, perfect but unspiritualized in his relation with nature until the Woman (Miriam, a young woman painter in Rome) ensnares him as an accomplice in her crime. The heroine of this romance (another young lady artist named Hilda) was perhaps intended to personify that "angel and apostle of the coming revelation" prophesied with such hopeless longing at the end of *The Scarlet Letter*.

The intent is breathtaking. The accomplishment, however, is like some improvident, undermanned excursion into a wilderness that will later be overtaken by inferior pilgrims carrying better maps and compasses. If Hawthorne had only acquired the disciplines of fiction that are commonplace to literally dozens of his inferior successors, this last novel might indeed have been the heroic rounding out of a life's work. Here was his great and chosen opportunity to fuse the diverse capacities shown in *The Scarlet Letter* and *The Blithedale Romance*.

Instead of being fused, the grand design crumbles into fragments we can ramble among without any compelling sense of direction. Where he should be writing a novel Hawthorne breaks off to write art appreciation, bound to start dating badly as soon as a new generation of tourists romped through the Roman galleries he was celebrating. He has put in extensive passages of travelogue, mere guidance to young ladies planning a trip abroad. Worst of all, again and again, the author keeps telling the reader what he is about to do without doing it, what he *is* doing without demonstrating that he is doing anything at all with his story, and what he *has* done without answering the reader's impatiently suspended question: How did things really happen?

Though it was published with some success and has had admirers through the years—some valuing it as a tourist guide to Rome, some for the ghostly promise of what it should have been—*The Marble Faun* is really no more a fully resolved work of art than the manuscripts of three other romances Hawthorne left incomplete at his death in 1864. The best we can say is that it was a big try. The big try is never a pure loss.

Hawthorne died on a journey. After his return to America in 1860, his physical and mental forces began, unevenly, with long periods of hesitation and the illusion of sustained health, to desert him. The nature of his illness is not known. He seems to have had a disease of the brain or spine.

He had returned to The Wayside with his family. He was famous throughout the literate world. He had enough works in hand to keep him busy through many autumnal years. But nothing would come right. The resolute cheerfulness he had maintained for his family's sake began to break up in periods of despondency. He was badly shocked by the death of a friend with whom he had taken a recreational trip. The outrun glooms of Salem haunted his mind again. He agreed to the suggestion that an excursion into the country might put him right. He did not return alive. Dr. Holmes, who saw him eight days before his death, speculated that he had "died by fainting."

After a century, the best of Hawthorne's work has only a thin coating of dust hiding its excellence from contemporary eyes. Even the most tedious and dated of his works are valuable to scholars and teachers seeking to bring what is good in them into an adequate light. *The Scarlet Letter* and half a dozen of the best short stories are essential to anyone's grasp of our history and present conscience. Hawthorne tried to bring the light and dark strands of American experience into a single pattern. The point at which he let go his effort is still the highwater mark of our insight into early American life.

R. V. Cassill has just completed a term as writer-in-residence at Purdue University, and he is also finishing a novel. His most recent book was a much admired collection of short stories, The Father and Other Stories.

Handsome and dynamic looking to the end, the Hawthorne of the last years is recorded in this portrait by Matthew Brady

One of the most serene and handsome regions of the United States lies along the Hudson River upstream from New York. It is also one of the most historically evocative and sturdily aristocratic. From the days when the great patroons and Dutch mercantile families settled the area—to be succeeded by English and Huguenot merchants, and finally by commuting businessmen—the counties of Westchester, Putnam, and Dutchess have been known as a domain of the wellheeled and the wellborn.

The oak and walnut parklands of the region are embellished with the lush country seats of Roosevelts, Vanderbilts, and Rockefellers. With its affluent towns and villages—Bronxville and Tarrytown, Pleasantville and even Valhalla—the area seems like an object lesson in the American way of life, a place where the American dream has come true.

Into this venerable neighborhood, however, there recently moved a new gentry whose influence on history may prove to be more profound than that exerted by all its predecessors combined. The newcomers are seventy men and women who form the Hudson Institute, an organization dedicated, according to its motto, to national security and international order. The Institute is located—some say aptly—on an estate that had originally been built as a mental home just outside the Westchester County town of Croton-on-Hudson. Despite the reassuring sound of its purpose—for who, after all, doesn't approve of national security and international order?—the Institute's arrival has provoked apprehension, even dismay, in the area and indeed throughout the United States.

The Institute is one of several such organizations which have sprung up since World War II. The Federal government, believing apparently that issues of war and peace are too important to be left to generals and politicians, is relying more and more on outside "think factories" for advice in planning domestic and foreign policy.

The best known of these factories is the RAND Corporation in California. This gigantic organization employs some eleven hundred people who deal mainly with the logistics of defense. They study cost analysis and the technical problems of defense—for example, how to deploy forces in a conventional war without exposing them unduly to the dangers of a surprise nuclear attack.

Another major think factory is the Institute of Defense Analysis, a smaller but perhaps more influential group located in Washington. It also deals with, among other things, the economics of defense, the cost of weapons and their efficiency—that is, which

WHERE THEY THINK ABOUT THE UNTHINKABLE

bomb makes the biggest bang for the smallest price? In some respects this institute is almost a civilian adjunct to the Joint Chiefs of Staff, and that, its detractors say, is just what's wrong with it. "Debate over its position has been intense," says one observer. "Many have resigned on both sides over its relationship with the Joint Chiefs of Staff." The I.D.A.'s detractors claim it is too closely bound to the military to be objective and is too vulnerable to attacks from special interest groups.

But it is the Hudson Institute above all others which seems to attract the greatest criticism, perhaps because of its nature. It is the only group that is occupied almost exclusively with high-level policy studies. Staff members recommend both in general and specific terms what should be the government

policy toward changing events abroad and at home. The Hudson Institute recommends policy; the others recommend implementations of policy. Of course this is not the only thing that the Institute does. Indeed, its members see their major function as one of exploring all facets of a situation; to them, the exploration is as important as the recommendations which may be derived from it.

The reports they publish, which analyze all actual problems and even all *possible* ones, must take account of a world where all things are possible, and most of them probably horrible. They might, for example, discuss what

to do if a Jew kills Nasser, Russia attacks Germany, Cuba or Indonesia gets the Bomb, ethnic minorities in North America attack the Anglo-Saxon Establishment, or a nuclear salvo destroys half of the American population. Their thinking is stimulated by considering such extreme problems as: What would happen if Mexico, supported by China, demands the return of Texas and California? Or if all Latin America united under an aggressive and belligerent dictator? Or if Quebec joined de Gaulle's Third Force, or, worse, under a strong leader turned into a northern Cuba?

Many people cannot quite believe that the way to avoid Armageddon is to plan for it, and the mere thought that someone is doing so makes them testy. The Hudson Institute's director, Herman Kahn, a mathematician, physicist, and master strategist for the Defense Department, has come under particular fire because of his cool and terrifying pronouncements about the future. "Many people just don't believe a nuclear war can take place," Kahn dispassionately remarks. "I do. I would judge it to be as likely as not that a thermonuclear device will be fired in anger before the year 2000."

Kahn is said to have been the inspiration for the character of Groteschele in the novel *Fail-safe*—a bloodless defense analyst who calculates in megadeaths; and movie producer Stanley Kubrick, although a friend of Kahn's, used him in part as a model

for Dr. Strangelove in the film of that name. In spite of this—or perhaps because of it—Kahn is much in demand on the lecture circuits where people listen in fascination to his blunt thinking about the unthinkable.

Kahn's detractors say the Institute is a nest of monsters whose preoccupation with the God-awful has turned them into cold machines quite out of contact with normal human emotions. One of them, James R. Newman, wrote an article in *Scientific American* which called Kahn's book *On Thermonuclear War* a "tract on mass murder: how to plan it, how to commit it, how to get away with it, how to justify it." Another critic, Anatol Rapoport, wrote of the defense strategists: "They are like butchers . . . and organizers of mass extermination . . . who . . . have a certain pride in

their detachment." On the other hand, the Institute's admirers call it "a reservoir of some of the best brains in the country." One prominent liberal, H. Stuart Hughes, called *On Thermonuclear War* "one of the great books of the century," and in *The New Republic*—surely no warmonger's journal—the same book was praised as "a contribution of real originality, humanity and intellectual courage . . ."

At the Institute itself, the members are proud of their moderation. They have, after all, done their best to discourage the paranoid approach to foreign policy which maintains that the Russians will destroy America as soon

At the Hudson Institute American strategists are working out policies to cope with every conceivable crisis—from a minor border incident to a nuclear holocaust

By BYRON RIGGAN

as they get a chance and that we must consider destroying them before they get to us. Compared with that point of view, or with the popular idea that we must respond to any Russian attack with an all-out nuclear reprisal, almost any other foreign policy seems moderate—including Kahn's position that someday, under a certain set of circumstances, we might conceivably make peace with the Russians by wiping out nothing but Moscow if they wipe out only New York. Of course, outside the Institute, many people are not inclined to think of this as moderation. And even inside the Institute there are those who would disagree with it. A number of the senior staff members maintain that although the bombing of civilians is a commonly accepted practice in warfare, it is actually immoral. One of them is even

writing a book with that point of view.

To find out which opinion of the Institute was correct, I drove north along the Hudson one superbly glowing day last fall. At a designated spot I turned off the highway onto a road winding among luxuriant trees and velvet greensward. Suddenly, the trees fell away and there, crowning a gentle hill, lay an enormous graystone English manor. A broad and graceful drive led to a parking apron where, in the distance, a pack of well-kept cars glistened like beetles.

I parked the car, shut off the motor and looked around. Somewhere an electric mower purred. The cicadas hypnotically announced autumn and the sunlight descended with drowsy benevolence.

Had I made a mistake? Could *this* be the place? In front of me, scattered across the lawn, was a group of young people enjoying a picnic lunch. The men were personable and the lovely young girls looked like recent graduates of Vassar or Wellesley. They all seemed very comfortable: the girls in sweaters and skirts, the men wearing tweed jackets with patched elbows. Some lounged on garden furniture; others simply lay relaxed on the grass.

I made my way over to the front door. At the reception desk a girl—Natalie Wood, it could have been—looked up from her copy of *The Politics of Hysteria* by Edmund Stillman and William Pfaff. She smiled as I introduced myself, and carefully scrutinized my credentials. "Oh, yes," she said, "Mr. Kahn is expecting you. He's out on the lawn."

Following her directions I crossed the main office: a high, vaulted room lined with filing cabinets marked SECRET. The thick rugs, the wood paneling, and the chandelier illuminating desks and typewriters gave the place an air of opulence and functionalism reminiscent of wartime England when ducal homes were made into offices.

I entered a long corridor lined with tall, slim windows and, on the other wall, with a series of doors opening into comfortably furnished offices. These rooms were full of squashy chairs and divans; large-scale maps draped the walls. A notice was tacked to one wall: "I came, I saw, I goofed."

From the corridor I stepped into the garden. Kahn, a fat, bespectacled man, sat in a chair surrounded by white hydrangea bushes.

"I'm glad you could come today," he smiled, indicating another chair. "I just flew in from California yesterday and I'm off for Chicago again tonight." This, I later discovered, was about his usual pace.

Our conversation came quickly to the point because Kahn seemed restive, almost poised for flight. This impression was heightened by his speech: a series of unexpected halts and spurts as if his brain outpaced his tongue. I asked him to explain the public criticism against him and he started speaking a mile a minute. "First let me say that few of my more virulent critics have read very much that I've written. They not only refuse to read me, but I'm told that some have refused to speak to me at cocktail parties. In part this is because they don't like to think about thermonuclear war. They think it is a self-fulfilling prophecy. You know about sympathetic magic? That's the belief that by discussing a problem you create it. If I sign an insurance policy, I spark my own death. If I go to be examined for cancer, I *create* cancer. *That's* sympathetic magic. But we think the most rudimentary intelligence says if you feel cold, put on a coat. When it rains, come out of the wet. Well, nuclear bombs exist. War is possible. We must think about how to prevent it or plan what to do when the bombs start to fall."

At that moment a tall, tweedy man appeared from behind the bushes. He had apparently overheard Kahn's remarks because he jumped right into the conversation. "Yes, people are, to use Henry James's phrase, simply tender minded," he said. "They mistake diagnosis for prescription. Viewing the world with objectivity, in all its colors, dark as well as bright, is not saluting nuclear war. But there you are. Some people would rather turn their back on it." This was Edmund

Stillman, former foreign service officer and author of several books.

How did the Institute get started, I asked.

"My colleagues and I," said Kahn, "thought it would be a good idea to have a high-level policy research organization, independent and nonprofit, committed to the public interest. We had the feeling that it should be detached, not an agent of government. In some cases we can actually mobilize more intellectual resources here on a problem than most government agencies can, because we aren't burdened with day-to-day decisions and problems. Here we can put five men on a problem for two years, and we do."

Work at the Institute, he explained, is done on a cost-plus-fee basis. Some projects are suggested by the government: the initiative for others comes from the Institute. Cost of the studies ranges from about sixty thousand to a quarter of a million dollars, depending on the amount of time, travel, and research involved. Ninety per cent of the work is done for various government agencies, and the rest for private

companies. For example, one of Kahn's books, *On Escalation: Metaphors and Scenarios*, was financed in part by the Martin Company, an aerospace firm. The Institute itself is nonprofit and uses payments for staff salaries and upkeep of the plant. Money that is left over goes for other Institute studies.

Despite Kahn's claim of independence, there is no denying the fact that the Institute's link with the gov-

ernment is a close one. Most of the private contracts that it signs involve firms that have an interest in military and space developments, and are, therefore, closely allied to the Pentagon. The Institute may be critical of the American "defense establishment," but it is an integral part of that establishment, nevertheless. That, its members might claim, is what gives their criticism its special value.

For the Institute is supposed to criticize the policy of the government. Presumably, it can do this quite freely for, so far as is evident, no one section of the government has any predominant influence on it. However, the Institute's motto is "national security and international order." As one Institute member said, "We are interested in keeping the world a place where our standards and ideals can be maintained." In other words, the main concern is, of course, the national interest of the United States.

Some staff members must, and do, have access to top secret information in Washington in order to formulate their recommendations. Kahn himself has direct and immediate access to the National Security Council, but not to the President. Some of the reports, bound in buff covers, are stamped CONFIDENTIAL, or SECRET, or TOP SECRET. Material is "confidential" if, according to Defense Department definition, its publication would "be prejudicial to the defense interests of the United States." It is "secret" if its publication could result in "serious damage" to defense interests, and "top secret" if its publication could result in "exceptionally grave damage."

"We've never had a robbery or an attempt at espionage, so far as we know. We've all been checked pretty carefully, and we could track down an inside job pretty well. And it's almost impossible for a stranger to get in here without our noticing it," one of the men told me.

"But are there really any secrets," I asked him, "that count any more?"

"Oh, yes," he said; "the cheapest way to make a nuclear bomb. Don't you think there are a number of countries that would like to discover *that?*"

I asked Stillman in what way the Institute differed from other groups of political scientists or military strategists. There's West Point, I thought, just a few miles upriver, supposedly turning out the best military strategists.

"In the past," said Stillman, "they have tended to work as individuals and not as groups, and of course, they were very often in military service—men like Liddell Hart in England, or Clausewitz in nineteenth-century Prussia. But there were no interdisciplinary studies, no team studies, no systematically organized group investigations of problems which brought to bear a wide range of professional skills. Up here we have scientists, historians, mathematicians, and writers, people with a wide range of backgrounds. We are by no means a monolithic organization. We often disagree. We have people here ranging from nuclear disarmament to preventive war—hawks and doves."

But most of the members of the Institute *do* agree about one thing, and that is the value of one of Kahn's creations: The Escalation Ladder. It is nothing less than a gigantic fever chart of twentieth-century international society, a list of all the major ways in which the world can go awry. Just as economists feel they now understand the broad workings of the economy and can control depressions, so some of the Institute people feel they can analyze the workings of international crises and perhaps control them. On the Escalation Ladder are detailed all the possible steps by which an original misunderstanding could be aggravated into all-out thermonuclear war. There are forty-four steps or degrees registered on the chart in ascending order of seriousness, from "Ostensible Crisis" through "Dramatic Military Confrontations," several degrees of civilian evacuation, "Formal Declaration of 'General' War," "Slow-Motion [intermittent] Countercity War," and "Civilian Devastation Attack," to "Spasm or Insensate War."

"And what," I asked Kahn, "is spasm war?"

"Spasm war is when the chiefs of staff press all the buttons and go home."

Our bright world tottering on the abyss? Our civilization moribund and plucking at the coverlet? Not necessarily, says Kahn.

"A spasm war on Europe might literally eliminate that continent as a historical force, but in a country as rich as the United States you might literally [this is a word Kahn is fond of] wipe out fifty to one hundred of the largest cities and a recognizable country would still be left over. What is left probably has enough wealth and skills and resources to enable us to rebuild in ten to twenty years."

In another study, which the Institute presented to Washington, it was stated that if a 50,000-megaton salvo were unleashed on the United States, the death rate would be almost 100 per cent even if some people survived the initial blast and remained in their shelters for *two months*. However, this unhappy turn of events is not likely to occur in the immediate future. It would take about fifty million pounds of nuclear warheads to deliver such a salvo, and it is highly improbable that the Russians or anyone else, including us, would have the ability to do that.

The Escalation Ladder really only measures the confrontations of major nuclear powers. The Berlin and Cuban crises registered rung nine on the Ladder. The Gulf of Tonkin crisis of 1964 reached only the third rung. The situation in Viet Nam is not even *on* the Ladder—because, according to the Institute, the United States is not facing a major nuclear power in this crisis; China is not yet considered one, and

Russia is not at this time confronting the United States over the situation.

But there is a step that goes beyond the top rung of the Escalation Ladder, beyond spasm war.

"You see," said Kahn, "we know how to build doomsday machines. It's not likely that they will ever get built, but it is engineeringly possible to destroy the world." I could think of nothing to say.

"It wouldn't be a bomb," he continued, "it would be a factory." By nuclear fission, the doomsday machine could pump out radioactive gas or material which would cause the death of vegetation, people, or anything else alive. Kahn says that it might take three to seven such factories built around the world to destroy it. The world, that is. It would be perfectly conceivable for the Chinese, say, to build one and then, if stratospheric currents were suitable, start up the machine to send clouds of radioactive material over the United States.

"It's hard to believe any nation would do it," Kahn added. "It's a very expensive project to build and it's very dangerous. If we knew someone was about to build a doomsday machine, I think we would be perfectly justified in launching a preventive war."

Going back to the more thinkable of unthinkables, I asked who would be left to rebuild after a spasm attack.

"It's possible that most Americans would survive," replied Kahn, "but depending on what we choose to do and what the attacker chooses to do, we could end up with almost everyone or almost no one surviving. But we don't expect a spasm attack, or any attack, really. Even if one occurred, there are likely to be weeks, perhaps even months beforehand, during which we can put in all kinds of programs that will make an enormous difference in casualties. The prototype really is Europe after 1933. A disturbed personality like Hitler got elected, and that was a warning. Then came other warnings: reoccupation of the Rhineland, the Anschluss, Munich. We think something like this is much more likely than the usual picture of buttons getting pressed all of a sudden and—*whoof!*"

When this encouraging speech was over, Kahn left me for a while after introducing me to Donald G. Brennan, who looked like a librarian but turned out to be a mathematician. His main interest was in arms control. He suggested we get some lunch, and as we entered the house he took my arm. "What concerns us is that more and more countries want the Bomb. This increases enormously the war possibilities. You couldn't, for example, trust Sukarno not to have used it against the Dutch if he had had it. Think of a Duvalier or a nuclear Lumumba. These prospects are very frightening."

No more so, I thought, than any of the other nightmares the Institute is concerned with.

We walked through a Tudor dining room and entered a small kitchen where food was laid out on a serving counter: cold cuts, pea soup, salad greens, lime jello, and cake.

"You see," Brennan was saying, "by the time you get weapons into the hands of people like Duvalier, they could get into the hands of gangster groups and they could be used as a form of blackmail *within* a society. You know; pay us a dollar a year per capita and we will protect your cities from being blown up."

I had seen a James Bond film which dealt with just such a contingency, and I started to say something about life imitating art until I remembered that *Time* magazine had called the Bond movies "comic strips for adults." But then, I thought, what does *Time* know? What do any of us family-occupied, bill-burdened, tradition-minded people really know about the grotesque horrors that lurk just over the horizon of the political landscape? How many, I wondered, really comprehend in their cortices and in their viscera that great cities and all the people in them can, in the blinking of an eye, be changed into specks of calcium, iodine, and carbon floating forever in space? Nevertheless, these

apparently calm and capable people at the Institute face the thought constantly with an imperturbability as bizarre as it is unnerving. Were there no inward bruises? No intimations of cosmic bereavement?

"We get used to it, like anything else," said Brennan, "but we have our moments. One of my friends in Washington committed suicide, but I'm not sure it was caused by his work. Our suicide rate is no higher than any other profession's. You see, the kind of person who is unable to meet this stark confrontation would hardly be drawn into a job where it's necessary to study the details."

What kind of studies are the most difficult? I asked. "Those which deal with post-attack recovery," he answered immediately. "Post-attack recovery!" For an instant I was reassured by the upbeat terminology.

Many of the Institute's studies and recommendations are secret, but information is available about the kind of thing they deal with. Some of the problems they have examined are: How do survivors form local governments in order to get society going again? In the aftermath of a nuclear attack, how will the ecology of the remaining humans be affected? How long will it take before plants grow again? Will plague and water pollution become a problem? This last is one of the few questions to which I could get a definite answer, and that was No, there would be no problem, simply because there will be nobody left alive in the areas of devastation where bodies pile up.

For obvious reasons, it is all but impossible for a layman to find out what many of the reports contain. One report, "The Role of Nuclear Capability in the Defense of Europe and the Strategy of the Pause" has a typically heavy-footed and recondite title that doesn't give much information away. Some of the contents became known, however, for the report was eventually cleared for publication. It recommended where to make use of nuclear bombs, how many to use, when to use them, and when not to

use them. It cautioned that the United States should respond in kind, after a conventional war maneuver by the enemy, and try to keep the war at a conventional level. In other words, *pause* before using nuclear weapons.

Even if the reports were open to reading by all, they would be almost incomprehensible, for they are written in a dreary and incredibly laborious style. It is as if the authors deliberately chose the coolest, most colorless words to counterbalance their hypercharged subject matter. Most are Sargasso Seas of print, stretching away to a fog-shrouded shore. For example, a study of the effect on arms control of civil defense measures reaches this conclusion: "Some of these lead to adverse effects which should be avoided; others may have a constructive effect that are capable of further exploitation."

Sometimes there are depth charges. A report that describes the effect of radiation from nuclear bombs comments on "fission products deposited locally"; "locally" means within a radius of *several hundred* miles from where the bomb falls. Another report, discussing the growing opposition to France's nuclear role, says that until now a common French view has been that, since a French nuclear force "could significantly damage the Soviet Union [the stock phrase is "tear off an arm"], the Soviets will not take a chance of a major aggression that would threaten France's most vital interests. The fact that the Soviets could kill virtually [or perhaps literally] every Frenchman in a retaliatory blow in response to the French attack, is often seen as of secondary relevance, although an increasing number of Frenchmen and other Europeans are beginning to believe it is of *major relevance*." (Italics mine.)

Finally, another example of a labyrinthine voyage through the murk: "It is possible to conceive of making strategic threats, the execution of which would be comparably painful for both the threatener and the threatened. Provided that the execution of the threat would be painful to the

AN ESCALATION LADDER

AFTERMATHS
44. Spasm or Insensate War
43. Some Other Kind of Controlled General War
42. Civilian Devastation Attack
41. Augmented Disarming Attack
40. Countervalue Salvo
39. Slow-Motion Countercity War

CITY-TARGETING THRESHOLD
38. Unmodified Counterforce Attack
37. Counterforce-with-Avoidance Attack
36. Constrained Disarming Attack
35. Constrained Force Reduction Salvo
34. Slow-Motion Counterforce War
33. Slow-Motion Counter-"Property" War
32. Formal Declaration of "General" War

CENTRAL-WAR THRESHOLD
31. Reciprocal Reprisals
30. Complete Evacuation
29. Exemplary Attacks on Population
28. Exemplary Attacks against Property
27. Exemplary Attack on Military Targets
26. Demonstration Attack on Zone of Interior

CENTRAL-SANCTUARY THRESHOLD
25. Evacuation
24. Unusual, Provocative, and Significant Countermeasures
23. Local Nuclear War—Military
22. Declaration of Limited Nuclear War
21. Local Nuclear War—Exemplary

NO-NUCLEAR-USE THRESHOLD
20. "Peaceful" Worldwide Embargo or Blockade
19. "Justifiable" Counterforce Attack
18. Spectacular Show or Demonstration of Force
17. Limited Evacuation
16. Nuclear "Ultimatums"
15. Barely Nuclear War
14. Declaration of Limited Conventional War
13. Large Compound Escalation
12. Large Conventional War
11. Super-Ready Status
10. Provocative Breaking Off of Diplomatic Relations

NUCLEAR-WAR-IS-UNTHINKABLE THRESHOLD
9. Dramatic Military Confrontations
8. Harassing Acts of Violence
7. "Legal" Harassment—Retortions
6. Significant Mobilization
5. Show of Force
4. Hardening of Positions—Confrontation of Wills

DON'T-ROCK-THE-BOAT THRESHOLD
3. Solemn and Formal Declarations
2. Political, Economic, and Diplomatic Gestures
1. Ostensible Crisis

COLD WAR

aggressor to be deterred and providing that the threatener has sufficient resolve, it is possible to conceive of

maintaining a posture of approximate or strict parity, even from a position of some strategic inferiority."

When, I wondered, do busy officials have time to read these reports?

In general, the reports indicate a series of alternative postures for the United States to take in varying situations. But others are quite precise in policy recommendations. One such is a report which was done by eight people and edited by Brennan, at a cost to the government of $145,000. It recommends that the United States cooperate with the Soviet Union on common civil defense problems. This is typical of the unconventional approach on which the Institute prides itself. The report maintains that civil defense is, in a sense, a war weapon. If the United States were to embark on the construction of a giant unilateral civil defense system, far more sweeping than anything we have now, the Soviet Union could regard it as a threatening act which upsets the *status quo*, in much the same way that Kennedy regarded the installation of Russian missile bases in Cuba. If so, the Russians might then feel forced to develop even bigger bombs to maintain the balance of power. So Brennan writes: "The President should . . . find it possible to say . . . that civil defense is good for the Soviet Union as well as for the U.S. on purely prudential and humanitarian grounds. . . . It would be substantially more difficult for individuals . . . to think of civil defense as a weapons system in a setting in which the presumed opponents had been encouraging and possibly even assisting each other in the

development of CD capabilities."

The report recommended exchanges of civil defense officials between the Soviet Union and the United States and a resident liaison man in each country. "In other words," it continued, "co-operative civil defense should . . . eliminate whatever arms-race aspects civil defense may possess." Then, in one of the few lapses from turgid prose, the tone became almost snappy: "Most of the exchanges of people that now take place between the U.S. and the S.U. involve artists. . . . While such contact *may* be important, it does not compare in importance with the dialogue that . . . takes place between people who do have some contact with the processes of government; aptitudes of Soviet citizens on this level are far more important than those of a Soviet ballet dancer."

It was now late afternoon, and I had only enough time to take a quick look at the War Games Room—really just a large conference room with maps on the walls. Here, men of the Institute dream up "scenarios," their word for hypothetical situations. Then they take the roles of various world leaders and argue out this mock crisis. The day I was there they had a brief conference based on the following situation: a United States plane in Viet Nam accidentally drops a bomb on Chinese territory. The ensuing

crisis went through various phases, and ended only when the man who was impersonating General de Gaulle maneuvered the rest into agreeing to a full-dress discussion of China's future at a later date.

Other, less easily resolved crisis scenarios can bring the world to a high rung on the Escalation Ladder.

One which the Institute has worked out grows out of the situation in Berlin:

1. Unrest and precipitating incident of violence in East Germany or Berlin.

2. A high level of popular agitation with street violence follows in East Germany.

3. The East-West German border (or the Berlin Wall) is opened up at various points by East German insurgents.

4. There is a limited but important degree of intervention by West German "volunteers."

5. The Soviets deliver a warning to West Germany and NATO.

6. Limited evacuations in Europe and the United States.

7. NATO replies to the Soviet warning with a warning against Soviet intervention.

8. Violence and border crossings

continue, with West Germans involved in large numbers.

9. The Soviets intervene, launching a limited foray across the border or initiating other major violence, or perhaps making a nonlethal demonstration of nuclear force.

10. Further exchange of messages.

11. A cessation of or abatement in hostilities.

12. "Armistice" is violated.

13. More evacuations and the initiation of other emergency readiness programs.

14. More border crossings by both sides.

15. One side issues an ultimatum.

16. Preparation and completion of emergency readiness programs.

17. Either the Soviets make a limited attack on Western Europe,

designed to display resolve and to split NATO (with the hope of gaining capitulation, or pressure for capitulation, by one of the major participants), or the U.S. makes a limited attack to deter the Soviets.

18. U.S. announcement of open cities and a city-avoidance strategy.

19. Similar NATO announcements of an open Europe west of the Rhine, with likely selective announcements of open areas in Germany.

20. Either the U.S. or the Soviets make a large counterforce strike with very careful avoidance of collateral damage, simultaneously issuing either a further ultimatum or an offer for a peace settlement.

21. . . . and so on.

This scenario employs some of the Institute's favorite strategic moves—evacuation of cities for safety or to indicate readiness for a showdown, demonstrating nuclear power without killing anyone, mounting limited rather than all-out attacks. Kahn and his associates believe that by talking through imaginary crises such as these, they can get a good idea of various responses that real leaders would make in a similar, but actual, situation.

Outside in the garden, we encountered Kahn again. Provided we are able to get to the year 2000, I asked, what will the world be like then?

"It's going to be an odd and interesting world," Kahn replied. "The per-capita income in the United States is likely to be ten thousand dollars per year or more. It would not be surprising if more than one half of the families have ten to fifteen thousand dollars per year of disposable income. This could well mean an aristocratic form of life in which we would be training children to enjoy themselves. You know aristocrats train children to dance, to enjoy food, to sing, and to play musical instruments. Also there could be enormous emphasis on skill and daring, and considerable participation in various sports. I think people will take—as aristocrats do—their avocations more seriously than their vocations."

And international relations in the year 2000? There was a long pause. "I can't capsulate that," he said slowly. "By that time, there could be fifty nations or more who may have access to nuclear bombs. It's difficult to imagine what this will mean."

"Quite an amazing man," said Stillman as Kahn rushed off to another appointment. "I think perhaps the most important notion he has come up with is this: because a button is pressed and a bomb detonated somewhere, that doesn't mean we must all commit suicide. All reason doesn't have to flee. I'm not denying that it becomes very difficult in the midst of all that din to hold onto reason, but that doesn't mean it can't be done. When a bomb falls, everyone should hold action. Ask before acting: Was it a mistake? Why did they do it? What do you think our reprisal should be?"

I asked him if, like Kahn, he thought there would be a nuclear war before the century was out.

"Yes, but it will probably be between two small powers, and the way it ends will affect the future enor-

mously. If one side wins handily, then that will be an encouragement for others to use nuclear weapons. If they massacre each other, then the nuclear deterrent will be enhanced for some time to come.

"We are in a completely new situation, a new world with no examples or precedents, and I see no long-term solution to world problems. I think we will do quite well if we can fend off any really destructive wars for another two or three decades. Then there will be new cards, new players, on the scene.

"For myself, I take a very gloomy view. I think civilization is a very chancy thing, that we live in a very precarious balance. I am always astonished at the progress made, rather than at the violence in the world today. It seems to me that no one can look at

RANDALL ENOS

the disorder today without a kind of pity. Not only for the Congolese, the Vietnamese, but for mankind—this wretched race of apes, if you like, intelligent apes, that does seem to get into trouble with alarming regularity."

I left the Institute as the staff was departing for home. The secretaries and researchers, released from their preoccupation with the horrendous, gaily called good-byes as they slid into their automobiles and, with an expensive whine of tooled precision, sped off to their homes in Westchester, Connecticut, and the East Sixties.

Driving back to New York beside the Hudson, that broad and venerable highway of American history, I realized I had forgotten to ask a vital question.

From the hotel room I called the Institute. One of the young assistants answered. "Have you prepared any recommendations," I asked, "on what we should do if the United States is occupied by a foreign power?"

There was a silence. "No," he said, "No, we haven't. You see, there is a law which forbids Federal money to be spent on any project which assumes the defeat of the United States."

I hung up and went over to the mirror. I spent some time looking at myself. Then I went downstairs for a giant, ice-cold, silvery Martini—shaken, not stirred.

Byron Riggan is on the staff of the Canadian Broadcasting Corporation. This is his first article for HORIZON.

Wreckers have demolished New York's Pennsylvania Station

MUST LANDMARKS GO?

The cost of preserving our architectural heritage is often high, and the past must compete with the future for a place in our lives

Although the cities of America suffer from a number of concurrent maladies (joint diseases in the sense in which I once understood this term), none now attacks the adrenal glands and the tear ducts of quite so many articulate people as the demolition of their older buildings. In some American cities—Charleston, South Carolina, for example—conservation of historic buildings has involved all good citizens for years; the same is true of New Orleans, where a dozen private organizations and public bodies have sworn to save the city's architectural treasures, by force if necessary. The vow keeps them busy. Elsewhere, until recently, the cause of architectural preservation enlisted only those history-conscious citizens who are likely to collect Bennington ware and tabulate the marriages of their ancestors. But it is fast becoming a widespread popular movement. The New Jersey Historical Society recently scheduled a conference on historic preservation; to the astonishment of some members, two hundred people came. Historic preservation is news. It became front-page news across the country recently, when the President received a report on the subject prepared by the special sub-committee on preservation established by the U.S. Conference of Mayors. The President was probably not in the least astonished to see that the preface to the report had been contributed by his wife.

Last year the first public hearing of the New York City Landmarks Preservation Commission drew an overflow crowd to City Hall; practically everyone begged the Commission to declare his favorite building a landmark. Few and muted were the owners who dared oppose such a ruling, though it might cost them money by making changes difficult and demolition nearly impossible.

Certainly anyone who wants to maintain precious architectural variety in the changing pattern of his city must welcome the rush of new volunteers. In a growing crescendo of protest, citizens in every American city are now seeking to prevent the destruction of older buildings whose *fin-de-siècle* lunettes and medallions afford a welcome diversion from the stark lines of modern commercial architecture. Yet it is relevant to point out that citizen armies are massacred more often than small professional forces. Countless foot-pounds of precious, unpaid civic work may be wasted trying to save from the wreckers those very buildings which are intrinsically beyond hope. Whenever private citizens pick a fight that cannot be won, the inevitable flattening of their morale makes it harder to rouse them for the next round.

The National Trust for Historic Preservation has probably devoted more thought and money than any other group in America to the saving of threatened old buildings. The Trust's officials meticulously point out that before citizens can win a battle to save a building they love, they need a careful evaluation of its merits. (Leslie Lane, a British authority on historic preservation and the director of his nation's Civic Trust, once told an American acquaintance that the greatest obstacle to preservation is misguided enthusiasm.) The American trust's check list of criteria poses twenty-one standards for evaluating a building. What, concretely, is its historical and cultural significance? Has it educational values? A capacity for public use and enjoyment? How much money will be needed to finance its maintenance and interpretation? Is a sponsoring group legally authorized to own and operate the building? Is its staff competent? And so on.

This recent surge of activity on behalf of the American architectural heritage must be somewhat puzzling to Europeans who were raised on the notion that America hadn't any. Certainly this nation lacks structures that the whole world accepts as hallowed masterworks; the best-known American buildings are new. Since older, pre-Revolutionary America was largely agricultural, the stately homes of the Washingtons, the Lees, the Madisons, and the Byrds stand, like Chambord and Blenheim, in the country. Sometimes they may be menaced by rural neglect and decay, but they are usually safe from the urban menace of housing developments, schools, and office buildings.

These new facilities, badly needed by new city populations, nevertheless threaten a significant architectural heritage very different from Europe's. The heritage includes a few town resi-

By ROGER STARR

dences, churches, and public buildings erected during the Federalist period of the 1790's and early 1800's. About 1820 Americans began to adapt popular European styles, the Greek classic and the Gothic romantic; in the cities there remain residential and commercial examples of both dating back before the age of Andrew Jackson. The cities also possess regional treasures, sometimes comprising whole groups or districts of similarly sized buildings of congenial style, perhaps notable less for their lines than for their details. Thus, the wrought-iron balconies of the Vieux Carré in New Orleans and, in the northeastern cities, the carved wooden trim of frame and brick houses, and the hardware of an industrializing nation: railings, lamps, door ornaments, and fixtures.

The American inheritance includes as well the technical innovations that merchant and manufacturer hurried to try. An outstanding example was the earthquake-resistant Montgomery Block in San Francisco, designed by "Old Brains," General Henry W. Halleck, later to become the Civil War version of today's Chief of Staff. Other examples are the prefabricated cast-iron fronts of the commercial buildings on New York's Broome Street, and the early skyscraper, such as Louis Sullivan's Schiller Building (Garrick Theatre) in Chicago.

The national treasure chest also includes the stately Romanesque or, more frequently, Renaissance villas which post-Civil War industrialists proudly set down between 1870 and 1910 on the broad avenues of the American Belgravias. In their roles as trustees or business managers, the same gentlemen also saw to the construction of large public and commercial buildings, frequently designed by the very architects who had planned their homes. Finally, the heritage includes those institutional structures, as Victorian as a crocheted antimacassar, in which enthusiastic eclecticism made a virtue of ugliness. Is there a soul too dead to swear eternal fealty to the hideous Jefferson Market Courthouse of New York, or the Company 15 Firehouse in San Francisco?

To satisfy their ravening needs, the cities have bit hard into this heritage. They are still hungry, and sometimes they seem to snap at anything in sight. In New York, all the palaces of the Vanderbilts have gone; so has Mrs. Astor's house, and Charles Schwab's. The Montgomery Block has gone from San Francisco, and the firehouse of Engine Company 15 has gone, too. In Bridgeport, Connecticut, a rare treasure of the Gothic revival, the Harral-Wheeler house, designed in 1843 by Alexander Jackson Davis, vanished as hastily as a gypsy tearoom. In Chicago the Schiller Building is down; so is the Rush Street house of Cyrus McCormick, noted for its heavy French accent; so, too, Marshall Field's house, designed by Richard Morris Hunt and the first house in Chicago to include electric light. Where not actually leveled, some older buildings are threatened with changes in their settings that will make them all but invisible. Thus, the citizens of New Orleans may be forced to choose between an interstate highway, vital to the city's heavy commerce, and an undisturbed vista from the city's Vieux Carré, vital to its personality and its tourist trade as well.

During the Depression, the Federal government established a painstaking study of the historical buildings of the nation. More than twenty thousand buildings were considered worthy of note. It is now estimated that between 1940 and the present day, more than 20 per cent of the buildings identified by HABS—The Historical American Buildings Survey—went out of existence. Some individual cities top the national average. One hundred and forty-five San Francisco buildings were covered in the HABS list; of these, ninety-five have been demolished, twenty-seven are still standing but are so changed that they are described as ruined architecturally, and only twenty-three are recognizable. The Historic Alexandria Foundation was established in that Virginia city in 1962. Its specialists catalogued 773 historic buildings. Within three years, by December, 1965, 11 per cent of these had been destroyed or desecrated, and 17 per cent threatened.

This trend has not only appalled local citizens and local historical societies. It has ignited such people as Ada Louise Huxtable, the architectural critic of *The New York Times*, and Wolf Von Eckardt, who performs similar services for the Washington *Post*. Some critics seem to have encouraged the belief that the destruction of older American buildings is always vandalism, unthinking vandalism. They point to the serene age of European masterpieces and chide America for not being able to save its treasures as lovingly. The comparison is effective, but unfair. The centuries that produced America's architecture were drastically different from those that produced the Parthenon, Chartres, St. Peter's, and Versailles. People just don't build palaces like Versailles any more. The concentration of available wealth and effort which Versailles represented, and which the other treasures represented in their own milieux, could be decreed only by cultural and religious institutions of central importance to societies that were themselves convinced that *something* must have central importance. By the time most American cities began to grow, philosophers had learned that kings possessed no divinity reliably different from that possessed by other men. Once all churches had achieved equal access to the truth, and the belief had gained currency that government was the servant of the people, not their master, a new Versailles became impossible. It can be said that the "better" the government, the worse, or at least the less interesting, became its architecture. The most important, interesting, and lavish buildings of the past century or so have been constructed not by governments, to celebrate themselves, but by private, nonreligious institutions.

Because the needs and uses of profit-making institutions change rapidly, it is difficult for their buildings to be maintained as part of the permanent urban landscape. Pennsylvania Station in New York City is a case in point. Whether or not one admired its style, it was one of the city's most impressive structures. But what does one do with an impressive railroad station which has ceased to be of use as a railroad station? In a dying city one boards it up and watches it become ruins; ultimately shepherds sit on its eroded columns and goats graze between the tracks. In a living city one first prostitutes it by making it into a more efficient machine for selling commuter and race-track tickets, and then into an architectural billboard by hanging signs, kiosks, and booths beneath its Roman vaults. Finally the day is reached when someone decides it is worth more as land than as structure and down it comes, to be replaced by an office building or a sports arena or both. I never heard one of the many objectors to the demolition of Penn Station suggest any profitable use for it.

On the other hand, government and religious activities, being less dependent on technology, change less over the years. One of the more beautiful structures in New York City, its city hall, was completed in 1812. The city itself has increased its population sixty-five-fold since 1812. Other buildings have been added to house new services, but the city has still only one mayor, and the city hall can still hold him.

This is a tribute, not only to the slow change in the forms of government, but also to the style and gracious dignity of the building itself. These gentle characteristics do not reflect the stormy conditions under which it was built. In 1803 the city of New York offered a prize of three hundred and fifty dollars for the best design for its city hall. Despite the modest architectural fee, the actual construction costs mounted so high in relation to the balance in the city treasury that the building was not finished for nine years. During all of that time contemporary citizens did not hesitate to suggest to the administration how their taxes could have been better used. Before a modern New Yorker views this infant democracy disparagingly through the lorgnettes made to cure a one-hundred-and-fifty-year-old case of municipal myopia, let him at least admit that some of the uses to which the city's money might have been put—hygiene, for example, or schools or street paving—might have been even more beneficial than the lovely city hall New York ultimately got.

Those who feel passionately about older buildings assume that every fellow citizen shares their view that the aesthetic and cultural value of a landmark building is supreme. Destroy their past, they feel, and the city's hope for the future dies with it.

Even if one is gloomy about the future, the facts, with some tragic exceptions, do not generally support the accusation of willful vandalism leveled against the destruction of an older building. No one, I believe, has suggested that New York's city hall be touched. But saving less singular older buildings may, depending on the circumstances, be a difficult assignment, even when the

buildings possess qualities cherished by respected cataloguers as well as the vocal public. In the first instance, it is difficult because the question would not arise if the owner had not already entertained the notion of demolishing it. Its owner customarily decides to demolish an older building in the expectation of erecting something new on its site. To calculate which is socially the more valuable—the present building or its future replacement—is not so simple as it seems to those who believe that the value of a landmark, any landmark, however defined, is supreme. Some of us may believe that if the values of the future building are understated in favor of an overestimate of the past, vandalism of another kind is being committed: unreasonable obstruction of desirable change constitutes vandalism against the future.

Why should an owner wish to demolish a landmark building to make room for something new? To make a quick buck, of course, the critics hiss, smugly criticizing those who have succumbed to a temptation to which they themselves have not been exposed. It turns out, however, that few landmark buildings are owned by speculators out for a quick buck. Those landmark buildings in the United States which are not government property are most likely to belong to foundations, societies, museums, schools, and churches (except in landmark districts, of which more later).

For the most part, these agencies have acquired the buildings by gift from their previous, or original, owners, or through another donor's generosity. The institutions use the landmark buildings for their operations, or, in some cases, they may finance their own corporate purposes with the income derived from rental of the landmark property, precisely as the benefactor intended. If they outgrow the building they use themselves, or if their corporate purposes require additional funds, shall they refuse to sell the landmark to obtain money for their needs? Shall New York's Society of Friends not try to sell its second, redundant meeting house, even if it is one of the city's rare Italianate 1860 relics? The Society needs the funds to expand its school to include a quarter of the worthy children on its waiting list. Are the leaders of the Society true to their corporate trust in refusing such an opportunity?

Having defended the right of corporate trustees to attend to

New York City Hall, often called the most beautiful public building in America, has survived intact since 1812.

their primary purpose, we must admit somewhat uncomfortably that the very nobility of that primary purpose may occasionally lend a glossy coat of respectability to the grossly improper. The First Presbyterian Church of Newark, completed in 1791, needing funds in the 1950's for its good works, and sensing that there was great public demand for parking space in the downtown business district behind the church, removed the bones of deceased communicants from its graveyard, placed them in a common trench, and covered the rest of the yard with asphalt which it divided into rentable parking spaces. This destruction of its graveyard, following upon several questionable brick additions to the stone church, demonstrated a curious lack of pride in the heritage of a fine eighteenth-century building. Yet, even while criticizing this, one should remember that the older sections of many cities are built, in part, on the sites of former burial grounds. In some American cities, large cemeteries within the city limits include tempting acreage of land which is somewhat underutilized by living persons. (Europeans have a less romanticized view of the disposition of the dead. There, public cemetery regulations frequently provide that graves are leased for terms of years, a practice that encourages re-use of the same space by a sequence of occupants.)

Even if aroused citizens can convince the vestrymen that they should not sell off their graveyard to raise money, a second difficulty is reached. What shall the vestrymen or trustees do with a church left high and dry by a change in the neighborhood or the departure of its parishioners? In a general sense, this poses the question, how does one keep alive a building whose owners have no further use for it, and which no one else wants to own, occupy, or maintain? A building is not an inert object of fine art, to be hung flat against the wall, or placed on a pedestal of modest size. A building needs care, maintenance, and use. Without all three, it rots.

The prospects for saving any single older building, and the wisdom of dedicating a major civic effort to it, may be calculated by attention to two basic factors which can almost be diagrammed on the axes of a graph. The horizontal axis might represent the re-use value, for other purposes, of the land on which the building stands. The vertical axis might represent the cost of adapting the building for a new use without changing its external appearance. Those buildings that are found on cheap land and are easily used, perhaps with hardly any conversion cost to speak of, would cluster near the crossing point of the two axes: saving them will be relatively easy. Citizen effort here is likely to be effective. Buildings, on the other hand, that are found on very expensive land, and present very high adaptation costs, would be located far away from the crossing of the axes on such a graph. Their survival potential is practically nil. Citizen activity here will be fruitless. Citizens should not be astonished to see that Philadelphia's urban revival began with the demolition of Broad Street Station. It occupied very valuable land, and at the same time no one knew what to do with it. On the other hand, small, abandoned suburban railroad stations may remain undisturbed for years. Even though no one knows what to do with them, the economic re-use value of their sites, along the railroad, is nothing. As a result, they are neither cared for nor demolished. A few, notably Henry

Some old mansions have been preserved by their conversion into funeral homes

H. Richardson's Chestnut Hill station outside Boston, are nationally known; others would be equally fascinating if their quaint architecture were not hidden beneath fifty years of dust and soot.

The important considerations for those interested in conservation involve the building which can be spotted near one axis but far from the other. Such a building might stand on cheap land, but be characterized by high adaptation cost; another might be cheaply adapted to a new use, but the high value of the land beneath it creates a demand for demolition and more intensive redevelopment. If either of these buildings is to be kept alive, interested citizens must find a way to increase its adaptability or to cut down the re-use value of its land or, preferably, both.

When challenged to find a use for a building they admire, most enthusiasts immediately think of turning it into a museum. In the large cities some of the first houses to be abandoned as homes did indeed become museums. Some of them celebrate the lives and times of the people who built the structures; others are merely a convenient repository of works of artistic or historic importance. New York's Jumel Mansion is a fine example of the first type; the Jazz Museum in New Orleans, located in a tiny Vieux Carré home, typifies the second. Decatur House, in Washington, combines the two ideas. But the limit on the number of useful museums is set by the number of worthwhile objects that can be put in them, not by the containers. Give us the champagne, we'll find glasses; give us great champagne, we'll make our own glasses. When important museums were recently needed in Los Angeles, New York, and Dallas, benefactors decided that converted mansions with inconvenient room arrangements and too many baths, pantries, and servants' halls would be less appropriate than wholly new structures. (One result of this drive for efficiency is the Frank Lloyd Wright-designed Guggenheim Museum in New York, a machine for viewing in which the visitor is treated like a loose ball bearing.)

I am not convinced of the practicability of turning a single old house into a period-piece memorial of the family living in it, unless the house or the family had some truly unusual and attractive individuality. Certainly the fate of the so-called Old Merchant's House in New York City is not encouraging. This is an early nineteenth-century, upper-middle-class home and business office. Although a nonprofit foundation has carefully preserved the building with the cultural artifacts of the times, not enough visitors come to the House to meet its operating expenses.

If the nation continues to suffer from a glut of museums, one can find a number of other uses for an old building by taking the trouble to look at the shape and style of the structure, or its location. Churches obviously can be, and have been, turned into auditoriums or theatres; the Jefferson Market Courthouse in Greenwich Village has, after great public organization and pressure, become a branch library (although the cost of conversion ran extremely high, judged solely as a library cost); a long-discontinued New York library, the so-called Astor Library, may on the other hand be turned into a theatre. The Syracuse home of C. B. Sedgwick, designed in Gothic style by Alexander Jackson Davis in 1845, became an advertising agency office, at least for a time; it has since been demolished. The handsome town houses of Henry

After half a century of neglect, Boston's Old Corner Book Store (1712), above, was saved from the wreckers. It has been restored roughly to its original state and now serves as a newspaper office, below.

Villard and his friends, designed by McKim, Mead and White, have for years been shared as office space by the Archdiocese of New York and Random House, the publishers. This successful adaptation was made possible by the location of the houses, directly across Madison Avenue from St. Patrick's Cathedral and in the heart of the New York "communications" district. The fantastically high land value beneath these low buildings would have doomed them long ago but for the fact that the party of the first part owns both the cathedral and the archdiocese. The cathedral, be it noted, never had a graveyard.

Most large old homes are not so fortunately situated as Mr. Villard's. If railroad stations, stock exchanges, and opera houses are the most difficult structures to recast for new uses, the next hardest category must surely be the mansions erected by families of supreme wealth fifty to ninety years ago. No single family, not even the wealthy progeny of the original owner, can afford to live in such a house today. High inheritance and real-estate taxes, as well as the servant problem, have often placed these buildings in the hands of specialized educational institutions. As these separate institutions become affiliated with major universities—a national and perhaps a world-wide trend—there are important

reasons for bringing the separate parts of the universities together. "Establishing interdisciplinary communication" is current jargon among university administrators who intend, in plain language, that all members of the faculty should share the same limp salad in the same faculty dining halls or clubs. This dietetic colloquy brings with it unexpected architectural consequences: the separate private palaces are to be abandoned; if tax-free institutions cannot use these structures, who can?

Giorgio Cavaglieri, a former president of New York's Municipal Art Society, has suggested that large corporations should make their headquarters in the ersatz *palazzi* of older American cities. He points out that the large European entrepreneur believes his company is enriched by locating its headquarters in a splendid Parisian *hôtel particulier*, or in a fabled locale like the Piazza San Marco. Mr. Cavaglieri suggests that American industry would derive similar benefits from locating its headquarters in, for example, Andrew Carnegie's copy of a Georgian mansion (now occupied by the Columbia University School of Social Work). Unfortunately, economics, like Mozart's *commendatore*, is knocking on the door. The aura absorbed from locating one's

headquarters in a genuine *hôtel particulier* (or in a Mies van der Rohe skyscraper), simply cannot be duplicated by locating in an imitation. The difference is approximately equivalent to the difference between Rembrandt's painting of the town council and the lithographed copy found on the top of a cigar box. No invocation or ballyhoo will cause either public or bankers to confuse the one with the other.

A few other uses may be found for these structures, but they are impractical unless their conservators can wrestle with the construction and fire codes or with the zoning ordinances. If these conditions were met, Mr. Carnegie's mansion might be divided into apartments with great charm and taste, and very high rents; something of this sort has been brilliantly accomplished with the Château of Louveciennes on the outskirts of Paris. Citizens might also consider the possibility of using such a mansion for any of the specialized institutions which cities need very badly: a pre-maternity home for unwed mothers is one.

Finally, one cannot turn one's back on the houses of the mighty rich without noting the interesting conservation of the Isham house in Chicago, designed in late French Renaissance style by

James Gamble Rogers. This house was completed for Dr. George Isham in 1903. After a glorious launching, it began to deteriorate with the death of its owner, until by 1959 it was nearly dilapidated. The savior of the Isham house was *Playboy* magazine, or more particularly its publisher, Hugh Hefner, who lives in it, having equipped it with a swimming pool, steam room, several bars, offices, a round bed eight feet in diameter for the laird himself, a billiard room, a motion-picture screening room, and numerous guest chambers which are taken over by an unbroken string of writers, critics, artists, players, and friends of Mr. Hefner. Not least, the building also contains a new dormitory for twenty-four young women who toil as Bunnies in Mr. Hefner's Chicago Playboy Club, or discharge administrative chores in the headquarters of his empire. Relying on the text of an article in a copy of *Playboy*, I understand that the young women from the dormitory have the run of the house and are permitted to sunbathe on the roof. Photographic evidence from the same source leads me to conclude that although Mr. Hefner has repaired Dr. Isham's furnace and installed air conditioning, a maladjusted thermostat must keep the building wildly overheated.

Playboy clubs are opening, or have opened, in many American cities and it would appear that at least one worthwhile architectural landmark in each might be saved from the wreckers by conversion into a dormitory-*cum*-sunbath for young ladies who work at the club. Without following this line of speculation further, one might simply recall that many of the most impressive mansions in the smaller cities are surviving through having been converted into funeral homes.

The case is considerably more cheerful when we discuss *older* single-family houses occupying sites which are in less demand for apartment-houses, and which therefore are better protected by zoning restrictions. Many of these buildings are saving themselves, especially if the land on which they stand was of relatively low value when they were built, before the Civil War. The low value of the land then meant that it had been built on by men of less spectacular fortune than those who built the monstrous later mansions to which we have already referred. The smaller, older houses on less treasured land tend to be of a size more nearly compatible with modern after-tax incomes and modern servants, or their absence. When zoning restricts this land to residential use, an entire historic district can be preserved, especially with the help of specific legal sanctions which forbid change in the exterior aspects of any of the buildings in the district. This applies the power of public law to enforce private covenants. These happy circumstances have helped to maintain the quality of old Charleston; of German Village, in Columbus, Ohio; of Georgetown, in Washington, D.C.; of Brooklyn Heights, in New York City, along with some streets in Greenwich Village; and, with some circumambient government help, of Society Hill, Philadelphia. But it is hopeless to confuse the conditions applying in such an area with the problems arising from houses too big for single-family occupancy today. And it is dangerous to overlook the second axis of survival calculation, the value of the land beneath the landmark.

The possible re-use value of the land beneath the landmark can be of two kinds. The first, and most serious, is the social value, which cannot be expressed simply in dollars: it represents the real need of the city or state to use the site for a purpose of surpassing importance. The claim that a certain parcel of land is essential to a public purpose has often been made on insufficient grounds—so often that some good citizens think it is never justified, that an alternative site can be found for any contemplated improvement. No appeal to generalization can settle the facts of any particular case. One can only point out that if an essential new need collides with an inalienable landmark, the landmark must be moved to another site. Some purists object in principle, but the surroundings of the actual site may have deteriorated so badly that the landmark may in fact have more historical significance in the new site than in the old.

In any case, whether one approves or not, landmark moving is an ancient human practice. Americans have made good use of it. Alexander Hamilton's "grange," or country house, a New York City landmark which, in all candor, is more talked about than visited, has been moved once; its survival depends on its being moved again. The charming neo-Gothic clubhouse of the New

York Yacht Club was moved from Hoboken to Glen Cove; now, moved from Glen Cove, it stands among other memorabilia of America's maritime history at Mystic, Connecticut. There are buildings in Williamsburg, Virginia, which were moved as part of the restoration, although the management does not call attention to it. The Georgian mansion of a British governor of New Hampshire was moved to New Canaan, Connecticut, beam by beam, some years ago. It looks fine in Connecticut. The Newark Museum includes in its garden the Lyons schoolhouse, moved bodily into that site by the WPA in 1937. The museum is now talking about taking over the Plume house, an eighteenth-century stone building reputed to be the oldest structure remaining in the city; long ago, the Lackawanna Railroad ran tracks through the building's back yard. It was used most recently as the parish residence of an adjacent church. The labor of taking the stones apart, moving them, and reconstructing them elsewhere will be colossal and expensive, but the new surroundings in the museum yard will be less incongruous than the present ones.

The severest menace posed by high land value to historic preservation lies in another direction. It lies in the fact that a fair return on the market value of the land can only be achieved by its owners if they rip down the landmark and replace it with another building producing the higher income that reflects the desirability of the underlying land. The simplest way of reducing this land value—or at least of attempting to reduce it—is by legislation. The New York City Landmarks Preservation law, for example, permits an owner to demolish a recognized landmark only if he is unable to earn a 6 per cent per annum yield on the fair value of his land and buildings. What is fair value? The law says that, barring special circumstances, the fair value of the property shall be its current assessed value for real-estate taxes, as established by the city's own tax assessors. This provision would mean that a landmark property will be regarded as producing a fair return for its owner even in the event that the annual return is considerably less than 6 per cent of the market value of the property. If upheld by the courts, this would successfully reduce for preservation purposes the value of the land on which a landmark stands.

Those who would save from demolition a fairly large-scale commercial building, like the Schiller Building in Chicago, or the Savoy Plaza or Sheraton East hotels in New York, cannot rely on this provision of law. The value of these buildings is too high. Great anguish has been expressed in New York over the demolition of the Savoy Plaza; a group of ladies of a type not generally considered revolutionary threatened to abstain from the purchase of Cadillacs unless the General Motors Corporation abandoned

A towering new structure will eventually rise on the site of New York's old Savoy Plaza Hotel.

A proposed new elevated expressway (foreground) would hem in the famous Vieux Carré in New Orleans

its plans to occupy a monster office building on the site, a building to be owned by a foreign consortium but bearing the General Motors name. The threat, incidentally, seems to have made little impression on Detroit.

I am not privy to the operating figures of the Savoy Plaza Hotel in recent years. Those who argue that the owners of such a property should be willing to accept less than the maximum theoretical profits from its land fail to understand the results of the current practice of fractionalizing the interests in such a parcel of land and property. If the same corporation owns both land and buildings, the argument that the owner should be content with less than the maximum profit makes sense. Frequently, however, the owners of the building have sold the land, perhaps to raise money for another building venture. The insurance company, bank, or investment trust that has purchased the land rents it to the owners of the building on it. The owners of the structure are faced, not merely with a theoretical loss of what they *might* make if something else were built on the land, but on an actual cash loss after paying the annual ground rent. Once the land value has risen to the point where such a sale is possible, no privately owned landmark is ever completely safe.

The citizens who want to save this kind of structure can do so only in general terms, by helping to prevent land value from soaring. They must help to control the economic redevelopment value of the land by putting zoning limits on the size of buildings. Effective zoning prevents a larger building from being constructed on the site of an existing one; in certain circumstances, it can require that any replacement of a present building must even be smaller than the present structure. Zoning ordinances, therefore, may effectively stimulate the re-use of an existing structure even if the interior must be extensively remodeled to turn,

for example, the Savoy Plaza Hotel into an office building.

Working for zoning controls is an educational experience in a city where great construction activity is tending to produce ever higher human densities. The construction industry—unions and management united—opposes restrictions that mean less work. The city's fiscal officer kicks because limits on the development of expensive land impose limits on the tax increases that the city might extract from bigger improvements. Everyone knows that a general zoning law, well conceived and directed to the encouragement of humane development, offers certain widespread advantages to the city. But few citizens recognize that good zoning is an effective, practical aid to the preservation of older buildings.

A precise example of zoning's ability to aid preservation can be found right down the street from my office. New York's recent new zoning resolution imposed a limit on the total floor area of any building that might be constructed in the city. This limit, as applied by law to the street intersection near my office, restrained the reconstruction of the easterly corner to a maximum floor area one-third smaller than had previously been permitted. The new limit made demolition and reconstruction economically unattractive, and this encouraged the owners of one of my favorite buildings to find a new use for it as it stands, rather than to demolish and replace it as had been done by owners of the buildings on the opposite corners before the new law was passed.

Looking across the small park behind the New York Public Library at 42nd Street and Fifth Avenue, one can enjoy the rare pleasure that this combination of new and old provides. Opposite one corner of the park stands the building to which I refer, a ten-story structure built for artists' studios some fifty years ago or more. The use required high ceilings which can be perceived from outside the building by the large horizontal windows, emphasized by decorative white lintels and keystones. Evidently the original owners of the building were proud of their investment, and both willing and able to use for the exterior walls a light-brown brick which contrasts with the white window lintels in a somewhat antique idiom. The owners have adapted this building for showrooms and photographers' studios. Many of the garment center advertising layouts are shot there. Across the street, a small new textile showroom constructed of white limestone or marble presents a low façade consisting entirely of vertical pilasters in grid form. To the right of this structure a small clump of older yellow-brick store buildings occupies the corner of the street. Behind them a new, moderately tall office building has risen, consisting mainly of dark glass horizontal bands, forming a contrast, though a muted one, with the buildings that stand before it. Behind this new structure, one glimpses the spiny roof turrets of older loft-and-office buildings in stone and brick. Across the street, on the right side of the vista, stands a new very high bank building, which, composed of setbacks that narrow as they rise, as simple in form as a stepladder, adds almost a humorous touch to the whole scene. The whole is characterized by precisely that unregimented harmony that provides the beauty of our cities.

For this, rather than attachment to the past, is what has stimulated the wide popular interest in historic preservation—the fear that the new buildings we will get from the modern economic system will be worse than those we are losing. It is easy enough to concede the blessings of corn flakes, canned soup, shoelaces, and homogenized pasteurized milk. On any given shelf these familiar and repetitious objects demand only a small arc of the eye's orbit. It is not easy at all, on the other hand, to concede the blessing of boredom in the urban landscape which surrounds and enfolds urban man as completely as the air he breathes. Under the twin pressures of high development costs and growing population, the heterogeneous urban landscape of the past is being chopped down; in its place grow large, simple-minded cubes of glass and metal, aesthetically inspired by cereal boxes, and, according to the critics, foreshadowing the time when each city will resemble a vast temporary army camp, built in a morning, and keeping within its boundaries only those who have been unable to get leave to go elsewhere.

A closer look at the urban landscape may indicate that historic preservation is not the only way to postpone or avert the army camp comparison. Municipal governments may be encouraged to produce more interesting and distinguished public structures. To do this will require the mobilization of dogged support for such generally unpopular measures as government extravagance, artistic highhandedness, and tampering with civil service protections, but it can be achieved, nonetheless. Private owners of new commercial buildings may be led to erect better new buildings in response to improvements in public taste. Accomplishing this will require tax incentive, *inter alia*, that will recognize as a special business expense the cash spent on architectural generosity. Progress may even be made in meeting the cities' severest aesthetic challenge: how to provide interest and variety in the vast residential construction that cities need now for their less affluent citizens. To realize this, however, will require a wholly new grasp of the potentialities, as well as the problems, of publicly owned housing.

We may perhaps take some measure of hope from the fact that people, intelligent, sensitive people, can frequently be wrong in evaluating the architecture and the city planning that is accomplished in their lifetime. Attend, if you will, to the familiar notes in this description of a growing city: "the rage of building has laid hold on such a number of adventurers, that one sees new houses starting up in every outlet and every corner of [the city] contrived without judgment, executed without solidarity, and stuck together with so little regard to plan and propriety, that the different lines of the new rows and buildings interfere with, and intersect one another in every different angle of conjunction. They look like the wreck of streets and squares disjointed by an earthquake, which hath broken the ground into a variety of holes and hillocks; or as if some Gothic devil had stuffed them all together in a bag, and left them to stand higgledy piggledy, just as chance directed. What sort of a monster [the city] will become in a few years, with those growing excrescences, may be easily conceived; but the want of beauty and proportion is not the worst effect of these new mansions; they are built so slight, with the soft, crumbling stone found in this neighborhood, that I shall never sleep quietly in one of them . . . "

These strictures were written in 1771 by Tobias Smollett, and they represent either his own view or that of a considerable body of Englishmen of conservative temperament. The point is that the city whose design so appalled Smollett and his contemporaries was not Gary, Indiana, or Calcutta, but *Bath*.

Almost two hundred years later, Lewis Mumford wrote of the very same city: "Even now, after a century and a half of change, the heart of Bath has qualities of design that even the best examples in Paris, Nancy, London, or Edinburgh do not surpass. The excellence of Bath shows the advantage of a strict discipline, when it is supple enough to adapt itself to challenging realities, geographic and historic. The placing of the Royal Crescent on a height that commands the whole valley, protected by the park that spreads below, shows that it was no mere application of an arbitrary geometric figure; and while nothing in the rest of the eighteenth-century city reaches this level of planning, the further building of Bath, right through the Regency, never fell too short of its standard."

Whether the contemporary judgment of our own city changes will seem more reliable two hundred years from now than Smollett's does today, we really cannot know. Perhaps the fate of his heated judgment may encourage current conservationists to remember that careful calculation is, in architecture as elsewhere, the key to survival.

As executive director of the nonprofit Citizens' Housing and Planning Council of New York, Roger Starr has for eight years advised, debated, lectured, and written about what is possible and desirable in terms of preserving a city's older buildings. This article is based on material from Mr. Starr's forthcoming book, entitled The Living End, *which will be published by Coward-McCann, Inc., in October.*

The Jefferson Market Courthouse in New York's Greenwich Village is being renovated into a branch library.

Watteau's chalk drawing of a flutist and two women is one of a large number of life studies that he made with no defined purpose in mind. These he kept in bound books, later using the figures in various combinations as models with which to people his painted landscapes.

WATTEAU'S FORBIDDEN WORLD

The witness of a life he could not share, one of France's greatest painters transformed reality into the most poetic and lyrical visions in the history of art

Eighteenth-century France, considered either as an ideal society devoted to pleasure and aesthetic cultivation or as a less than ideal society given over to libertinage and dilettantism, had its life-span shortened at both ends. Beyond term and groaning not with labor pains but with boredom, it had to wait for Louis XIV to die—fifteen years after 1700—before it could be born, and it lost its last decade when another society put it to the guillotine. "Do get on with it—things are so dull," the court might have said to their dying monarch; three-quarters of a century later Mme du Barry cried out on the scaffold, "One moment more—life is so sweet!"

Three painters neatly spaced into successive generations—Watteau, Boucher, and Fragonard—recorded the ideal promise, the surface triumph, and the lively decline of this society, without introducing so much as a hint that it was faulty and threatened by revolutionary philosophies. At its end, when the foundations were eaten away, Fragonard was still romping exuberantly about in the decayed structure as if it were perfectly sound; although we, by forcing hindsight a bit, can read into his art the symptoms of the fall, no world on its last legs has ever been presented more attractively by a participant who enjoyed its pleasures with less question.

Earlier, Mme de Pompadour had had the perception to make her sinister prophecy "*Après nous le déluge*," but that lady's favorite painter, Boucher, offers nothing more revealing than skillfully enameled surfaces celebrating the niceties (with an occasional lapse into the vulgarities) of established taste. Eighteenth-century France found no social critic among artists, as did eighteenth-century England in that vigorous protestant against the evils of the day, Hogarth. But France did find an artist great enough to distill the virtues of its privileged society into an ideal expression. He appeared early, during the first decade of that so-

By JOHN CANADAY

61

Watteau: Seated woman, *crayon*

ciety's existence, but remained an observer from outside, as if he sensed that the corruption inherent in the ideal must affect anyone who was fully a part of the game. This outsider was Jean Antoine Watteau.

All Watteau's surviving paintings were done during the last twelve years of his life, which means the six years before the death of Louis XIV and the six after. The chronological sequence of these paintings cannot be worked out with much certainty, but Watteau's mature style, the apotheosis of the century's ideal, was born during the middle years of the twelve from the conjunction of three circumstances: the death of the old king and the consequent release of the new century; Watteau's adoption as protégé by the immensely rich Pierre Crozat, which placed him in a position to observe the new society intimately; and the appearance of the first strong symptoms of tuberculosis, which intensified the poignantly withdrawn nature of his spirit (and which eventually killed him at the age of thirty-six).

Surely we may assume that the dreamlike quality of Watteau's art—its quiet, half-melancholy languor, the impression it gives of having been created by a nonparticipant from an observation point just outside the borders of life—is connected with his frailty. He seems to understand what the passions of men and women are, yet he

must reduce the tempests of physical love to a sweet, regretful tenderness. The sexual games are refined to graceful suggestions: the bacchanal becomes a stroll in a shaded park; the delights of the flesh are recognized and perhaps yearned for, but their consummations are abjured from the beginning. The murmured endearment must do for the amorous lunge, even for the caress. When a lover occasionally yields to impulse and commits a preliminary *faux pas*, he disrupts the reconciliation between abstract desire and physical potential that holds Watteau's world together so harmoniously, but so tenuously, against all the natural violences of life. It is a nostalgic world whose fragile denizens, shimmering in taffetas and satins as they wander through it, seem to look back upon the fullness of lost pleasures that, in truth, they have never experienced.

It is odd to discover from comments made by his contemporaries that this most poetic artist of the eighteenth century was thought of as a realist. Etienne Jeurat, a genre painter who engraved some of Watteau's works, could make the closest possible translation of these almost ethereal visions and still admire Watteau as a painter who "marvelously imitates nature." If the comment seems implausible to us, who have seen the nineteenth century's demonstration of what the close imitation of nature can mean, it does make us look at Watteau a second time from

Watteau: Girl on a swing, *pencil and chalk*

a different angle and calls our attention to an element in his art that we take for granted. In one context of his time, Watteau was not only a realist but innovational in his realism. He anticipated the impressionists' use of the visual world as one vast snapshot, whose bits and pieces could be painted (with no matter how much calculation) to reveal the essential character of a scene, a person, or an object, through its casual surface. If Watteau's world is an invention and a lyrical dream, and if the people who move within it are variants of a human race more fine-boned than birds and as exquisitely plumaged, he pictured that world as the impressionists pictured theirs, in its momentary, unself-conscious aspects, with its denizens unknowing, or not caring, that they are observed.

Watteau's genius for observing the casual gesture—the turn of a head, the lift of an arm, the stance of a body as it conforms to the balances of walking, sitting, or playing a musical instrument—and his sensitivity to these unstudied attitudes as revelations of mood and character are apparent throughout his paintings, but such gestures are most wonderfully set down in his drawings. He made of drawing something that it had never been before, something barely related to his contemporaries' idea of drawing—in terms of musculature academically rendered, of the invention of posturings and proportions in which the

body becomes a machine adaptable to the contrivance of compositions in the grand manner—or indeed to the idea of drawing as a memorandum of facts for later reference. Even genre painting, with its basic premise of echoing daily life, was a matter of setting a typical, explanatory, narrative pose, which in being once removed from the spontaneously assumed attitude might be entirely removed from immediate perception and expression.

Watteau was so indifferent to these conventions, so alone in his use of drawing as the expression of intimate response to observed objects, that twenty-seven years after his death, in a lecture before the Academy, his good friend the Comte de Caylus asserted that Watteau "knew nothing about anatomy" because he seldom drew from the nude. But no draftsman has more beautifully integrated the structure and movement of a body, clothed or unclothed. Caylus could refer to Watteau's "inadequacy in the practice of drawing" only because Watteau did not draw in the heroic manner.

No doubt it is true that if Watteau had attempted heroics he would have been lost, but nothing could be more beside the point. With the possible exception of the eccentric Renaissance Italian Jacopo da Pontormo, who is in a class outside any other, Watteau is the first modern draftsman, the first artist whose informal sketches

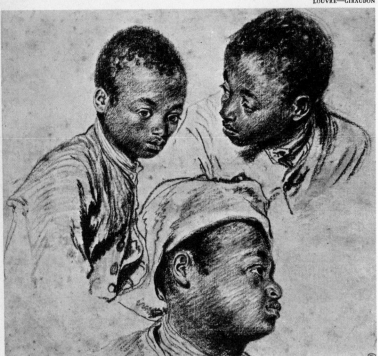

Watteau: Studies of the head of a Negro boy, *chalk and wash*

can be appreciated in terms of an independent art that is as revelatory as painting. Yet even here, in his most personal work, Watteau holds himself aloof. He is the most sensitive of observers, but never a participant.

His physical frailty aside, Watteau was always temperamentally an outsider. He had many acquaintances, but they were persons who had to seek him out. He had no intimate friends, and he never married; if he had any serious love affair, there is no record of it in the accounts of people who knew him and would have had no hesitation in mentioning an attachment that could hardly have escaped their attention. Solitary by nature, during his successful years Watteau moved in a company that included some of the most conspicuous men in France, men who were powerful, ambitious, and close to the court—hardheaded and sometimes unscrupulous. In a fashionable world of exquisite niceties and sexual intrigue his paintings set fashions in dress if not in comportment. He certainly was aware of the ferocity and cynicism that coexisted with the ideal of polished sensitivities and delicate refinements, and he knew also the world of the streets, the fairs, and the hand-to-mouth existence that during his earliest youth he shared with other starveling artists.

With this top-to-bottom material at hand, an artist of different temperament could have been a French Hogarth, but the contrast between Hogarth and Watteau is so extreme as to be almost pointless. Hogarth's power was his ability as a social commentator to expose the worms beneath the veneer. Watteau's greatness was that he legitimized the surface by treating it not as an ideal that had anything to do with a real society but as a poeticized state of being.

The importance of Watteau in our appreciation of the

TEXT CONTINUED ON PAGE 73

A GRAVURE
PICTURE
PORTFOLIO

The paintings reproduced on the following eight pages, all done within a relatively few years, represent the quintessence of Watteau's genius as a painter. According to one of his patrons, Watteau was only rarely satisfied with his own canvases. Today these are considered, almost without exception, to be among the most memorable creative achievements of the eighteenth century.

GILLES, 73″ x 59″

THE EMBARKATION FOR CYTHERA, 51″ x 76½″

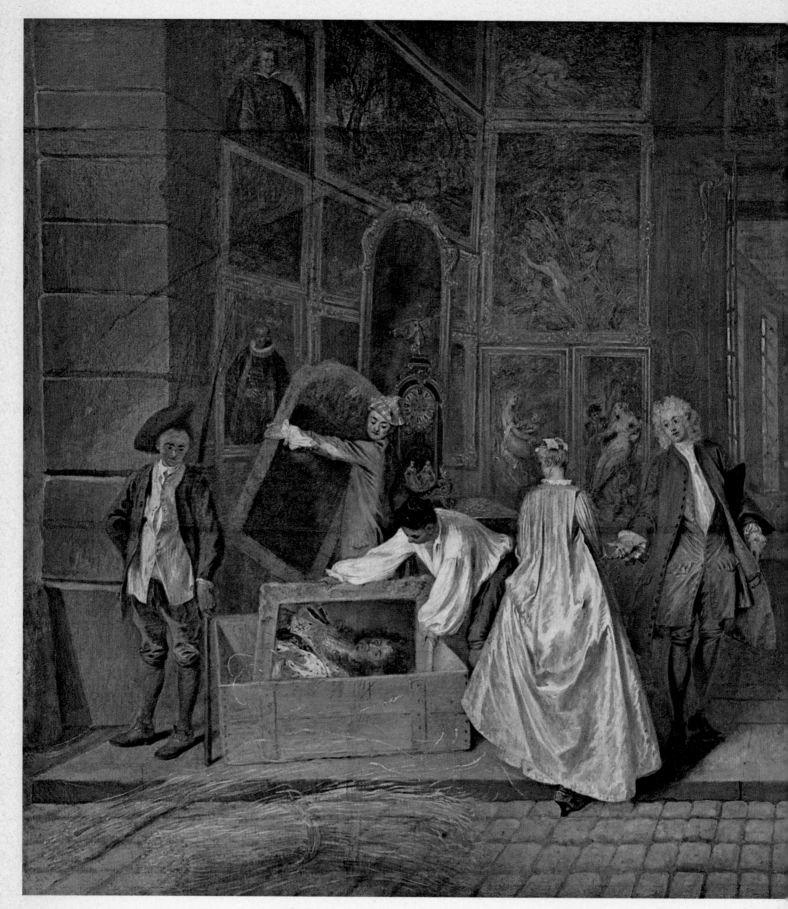

THE SHOP SIGN OF GERSAINT, 63" x 120"

THE MUSIC PARTY, 25″ x 36″

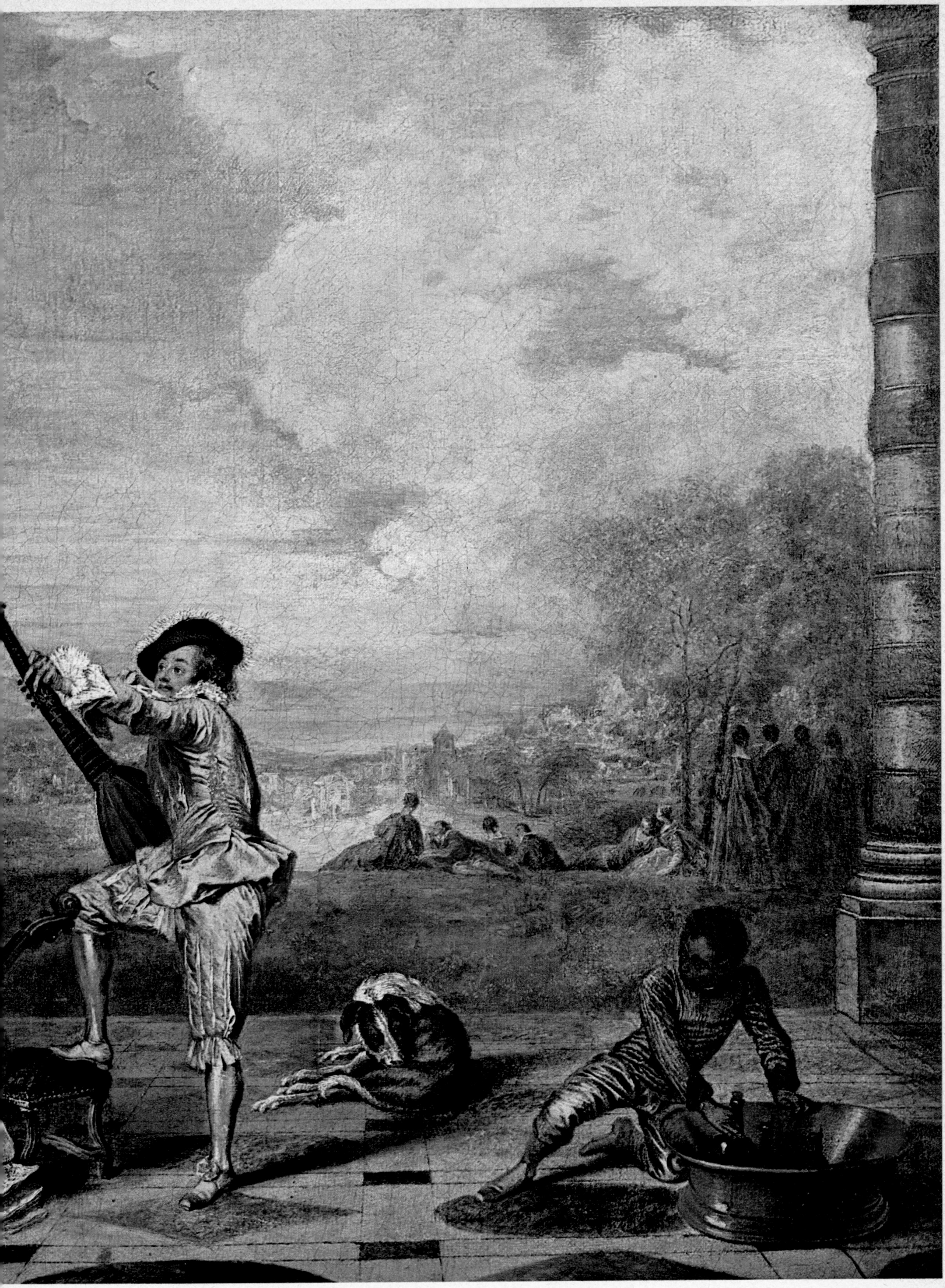

COMPLETE ACCORD, 13½″ x 11″

eighteenth century is greater than we realize. Without him we would have only a record of courtly affectations in the works of Boucher, of licentious charm in those of Fragonard, of modes in portraits and popular prints and, in Gainsborough's canvases, an affectionate revelation of the natural warmth that exists in good people beneath frivolity and fashion. Without Watteau, Gainsborough would remain the century's greatest painter; but even Gainsborough, for all his poetical touch, loses his essence if we try to regard him as much more than a single favored spokesman of eighteenth-century England. Watteau alone abstracted from the froth of his century an essence that, for all the particularity of its raw ingredients, rises above time and place.

*W*atteau was born within the seventeenth century, on October 10, 1684, and was little more than nominally French by origin. His parents were Flemish and his natal city, Valenciennes, had been French for only six years at his birth. But Watteau was the artist who revised French painting, shifting it quite suddenly from the seventeenth-century formalism of Poussin and Le Brun to a kind of Parisian Frenchness that has ever since been a steady dominant in French art. It is a Frenchness best understood by most people in the art of Renoir, a Frenchness where gaiety and tenderness are perfectly matched, where casual diversions are understood as manifestations of the good things that each individual experiences, or hopes to experience, within the intimacy of his own life.

Watteau's father was a master tile and slate craftsman of unstable temperament, given to violent rages and probably an alcoholic. Tax records classify him as a bourgeois, so he must have been literate and, within his craft, prosperous enough. There is no way of reconstructing Watteau's childhood; legend appropriately makes it an unhappy one. He chose his own métier as painter and was apprenticed at fifteen to one Jacques-Albert Gérin, an obscure pedant. When he was only eighteen he found his way to Paris. This early departure from home suggests that things were in fact not too happy there.

Penniless and alone, Watteau attached himself to a group of Flemish painters who ran a workshop on the Pont Notre-Dame, where souvenir paintings were ground out by the gross, like postcards, for sale to wholesalers from the provinces and peasants who came to town for the fairs. Watteau's specialty was Saint Nicholas. He received virtually no pay—a few francs and a soup ration.

Slight of build, of medium height, reserved or even timid in manner, and indifferent or helpless in practical matters, Watteau was frequently underpaid or cheated, but he so inspired the protective instinct in others that from his late teens on he was befriended by a series of dealers, fellow artists, and collector-patrons who form in retrospect a kind of "Watteau Benevolent Society." He

lived in their houses or studios, coming as a welcome guest but never staying long, moving out for reasons not explained. In the reminiscences of people who held him in affection, Watteau's carelessness, his untidiness, his impatience, and his fits of misanthropy and withdrawal are accepted as corollaries to his talent, and even as part of his charm.

But Watteau was not a charmer by intention. He was an archetype of the kind of artist, familiar today, who has replaced the hard-working supercraftsman of the Middle Ages and early Renaissance, the god-philosopher of the high Renaissance, and the practical man of affairs of the seventeenth century. He was the artist as a man not quite like the rest of us. His inability to cope with the world is inherent in a talent that must be nurtured and protected, and those who discover and patronize that talent are rewarded by the satisfaction of vicariously sharing his creative gift. Watteau's patrons were that special type of *amateur* peculiar to the eighteenth century—professional men, financiers, or dilettantes whose avocation was patronage and collecting and who might enjoy the practice of an art, usually painting or engraving, as a serious hobby.

Watteau came into this circle by stages. The year after his arrival in Paris—he was now nineteen—he was befriended by a dealer and print publisher named Jean Mariette, who had a shop in the rue Saint-Jacques. Mariette let Watteau study his stock of prints by Jacques Callot, and engravings after Rubens and Titian. There were probably drawings by all three, as well. Callot's superb theatricality, Rubens's radiant glorification of color (and of the flesh), and Titian's poetization of all sensuous experience were to become the major outside influences in the expression of Watteau's genius. The impact of Callot was immediate, in conjunction with a firsthand acquaintance with the *commedia dell' arte* that Callot had celebrated. But at this time, in a Paris that was not yet the city of public museums, Watteau must have seen very few paintings by Rubens and perhaps none by the Venetians. That had to wait until he knew the important collectors.

Mariette probably brought the young artist to the attention of Claude Gillot, with whom Watteau worked from about 1704 to 1708, still at the level of apprentice and assistant. Gillot, who was Flemish and a rebel against the academic doctrines, painted lively scenes of Parisian life and designed sets for the *commedia*. Louis XIV had banished the Italian players for their satire on the prudery of his Mme de Maintenon in a piece called *False Chastity*, but the Italian tradition was carried on by French actors who became popular idols at the same fairs where Watteau's little hack paintings of Saint Nicholas were sold. As a friend of Gillot's, he must have met the actors and must have sketched them during rehearsals or performances, but no record of this has survived. For that matter neither do the bawdy high spirits of the *commedia*

Watteau: Nude half-figure with raised arm, *chalk*

that delighted Callot survive in the later paintings in which Watteau echoed the theatre. The *fêtes galantes,* Watteau's final and greatest works, evoke the grace and high style of the comedians, but the mood shifts into a key of dream and regret. Where the references are specific, as in *Le Mezzetin* (cover) and the portrait of *Gilles* (page 65), the models were not actors but friends of Watteau's who posed in the theatrical costumes that he kept in his studio.

When he was twenty-one, Watteau met Jean de Julienne, a young man of the same age who was the manager (and later, by inheritance, the owner) of his uncle's prosperous textile factory. For the rest of Watteau's life, Julienne did his best to keep the artist's affairs in order for him. But it is important to remember that in the world represented by Julienne, Watteau was never a careerist. His gratitude to his friend-patrons accounted for the concessions he made in the socializing that went on. He was interested in the Comte de Caylus, another friend his own age, and yet another well-placed friend, Nicolas Henin, superintendent of the king's buildings and gardens, more because they met to draw from the model than because these companions moved in the great world, or close to it. Julienne also, as an *amateur,* was a painter, engraver, and musician.

At the age of twenty-four, Watteau for the first time came into something like a position of security, when he joined Claude Audran, a popular decorator, as assistant. Still trying to find his way as a painter, he competed unsuccessfully for the *Prix de Rome* with a picture, since lost, on an assigned subject that could hardly be less suggestive of his spirit: *David's return after defeating Goliath.* The impression made in these years is one of Watteau waiting for self-discovery; and of Paris waiting for the court to abandon Versailles so that it could flower into a city of elegant town houses and high living.

*I*t is not known exactly when Watteau met Pierre Crozat, but with that meeting began the full realization of the Watteau we know. Crozat was not quite the richest man in France, but his brother Antoine was so rich as the result of his monopoly of the Louisiana trade that he was never able to estimate his wealth. (Antoine was called "*Crozat le riche,*" and Pierre, "*Crozat le pauvre.*") But Pierre was rich enough. He was in his fifties when he met Watteau, and at forty-three had retired from business and purchased at a steep price the office of Treasurer of France, with all the advantages involved. His palace and gardens in Paris were on the royal scale. He staged concerts and theatricals there for his friends. His parties were famous, and although they seem to have been more sedate than the outrageous drunken revels of the aristocracy (for instance, the routs of the Duchesse de Berry, which, as described by her contemporaries,

were imposing in their debauchery), they could hardly have been given over entirely to aesthetic cultivation. Intrigues for power must have occupied the influential men who gathered in the halls of this palace. And the gardens, where the guests strolled after the concerts, were a perfect setting for the maneuvers of amorous dalliance.

Crozat probably met Watteau through the dealer Sirois, one of the most important members of the "Benevolent Society," in whose house Watteau was living at the time. In 1715 or 1716 Watteau moved out to occupy an apartment in Crozat's palace. Crozat was an avid collector (and on the side, informally, a dealer who picked up treasures for his collector friends). Among his five hundred paintings and nineteen thousand drawings there were, as a single breath-stopping example, about twenty-five paintings and three times as many drawings by Titian alone.

Watteau was now surrounded by the paintings that were his true teachers, and he had access, through Crozat, to the royal collections as well. While Crozat set about making him a fashionable painter, Watteau watched the gallantry of the garden parties that gave him his nominal subject matter, but it is difficult to think of him as part of the company. If he mingled, he remained psychologically removed, and after a year or so he left the palace. There was no break with Crozat; Watteau probably moved out because he wanted to get away from distractions that were imposed upon him as a reluctant and increasingly ailing participant in a kind of life for which he had neither taste nor energy.

Before long he was sharing quarters with Nicolas Vleughels, a successful copyist who seems to have been as close a friend as Watteau ever allowed himself. Still unknown to the general public, Watteau had become the favorite painter of Crozat's circle, so popular, indeed, that Vleughels's copies of his paintings were sold before they were finished. But he was still a bit of a wildcat artist under a system that required acceptance in the Academy not only as a matter of prestige but as a form of official union card in the professional hierarchy. He had been an Associate of the Academy for five years, meaning that he had been given permission to offer a painting to be judged for full membership. But with typical dilatoriness he had never got around to producing the large showpiece on the standard pattern that was expected. Crozat urged him to follow through with this, and no doubt also set about dropping a word here and there to assure in advance a properly sympathetic reception for his protégé.

In 1717 Watteau was accepted into the Academy with the *Embarkation for Cythera* (pages 66–67), his masterpiece but a most unconventional presentation piece. With its gentle lovers strolling toward a gilded confection of a

Bath of Diana by Boucher (below, detail above) is a typical example of this artist's erotic nudes. Although as a youth he studied Watteau's drawings and made engravings of them, compared to the latter's lyrical essays Boucher's figures are sensual, earth-bound, and unfailingly decorative.

LOUVRE—GIRAUDON

75

Lancret: Picnic after the Hunt

boat that will carry them to the realm of love—Watteau's transmutation of the byplay of seduction—this poetic vision had nothing to do with the declamatory rhetoric expected of a candidate, and the Academy had to create a special category for Watteau: "Painter of *Fêtes Galantes.*" In the war between the Poussinists and the Rubensists that divided the academicians, Watteau's election was considered a victory for the Rubensists; and so it was, for the fastidious Watteau and the robust Rubens, paradoxically, had much in common. But it was more important in a way that was not noticeable at the time. A new force outside the Academy had challenged its dictatorial powers; the regime of the private patron and the personal artist had begun. Although Watteau's election with so unconventional a painting involved no preliminary skirmish, the skirmishes were to occur and grow more and more frequent until finally the Academy's defeat by the impressionists and their patrons would break its power forever.

Watteau was thirty-three when he painted the *Embarkation.* Two years later he was so ill that he went to Lon-

don to consult Dr. Richard Mead, the queen's physician, and was there subjected to such treatment as the best medical knowledge could provide. He returned within months to find that the good Julienne had managed his affairs so well that he had accumulated some money in spite of the panic caused when an outgrowth of Antoine Crozat's speculations in the New World, the fabulous "Mississippi Bubble," burst that year.

Now he moved in with his friend Gersaint, who, as the son-in-law of his old dealer, Sirois, had taken over the business. In gratitude Watteau painted for Gersaint the famous signboard that rivals the *Embarkation* as his finest work (pages 68–69). It shows the interior of the shop as if seen from the street with the front wall removed—customers are being received, others are examining paintings, workmen are boxing a portrait for shipment. Divided between genre and poetics—or, rather, fusing the two—it is the unique example in Watteau's work that might justify for us the label of realist that seemed appropriate enough to his contemporaries.

Early in 1721 Watteau left Paris for Nogent-sur-Marne,

Pater: Gathering of *Commedia dell' Arte* Actors in a Park

where he hoped the air would help him. (He stayed on the estate of Philippe Le Fèvre, Master of the King's Table.) But he knew he was dying. The extremity of his illness seems to have caused a change in his character. His friends had noticed, upon his return from London, that he had become avaricious. With his life ebbing, he became concerned about the practical future. For the first time he complained about the prices his paintings fetched. He had never given any indication of worrying about his soul: now another future also concerned him. He painted a *Christ on the Cross* as a gift for the local curé, and destroyed a number of paintings and drawings that he feared were erotic. (Both Caylus and Gersaint, in recollections after Watteau's death, referred to a "libertine spirit" repressed beneath the purity and caution of his comportment.) He died in the arms of Gersaint on July 18, 1721, three months before his thirty-seventh birthday.

Immediately after Watteau's death, Julienne began the compilation of all his existing works—pictures, drawings, and the decorations he had painted as assistant to Audran

—in the form of engravings. This was the monumental tribute and record called the *Recueil Julienne*. It was not until this work appeared that Watteau became known to anything like a large public. It also made his work an international influence on painters for the rest of the century, although only to the extent that they adapted his subjects or copied his motifs. He had achieved the ideal statement of a far from ideal society during a single decade of its existence, and in spirit he found no followers.

In actual practice, however, he found two, both a few years younger than he: Jean Baptiste François Pater (1695–1736) and Nicolas Lancret (1690–1743). Pater was by birth Watteau's fellow townsman, by training his pupil, and by intention his second self in art, copying his style as well as literally copying his paintings. During the last years of Watteau's life he and Pater were reconciled after a quarrel, and apparently he regarded Pater as his aesthetic heir. But Pater was often a careless painter and, in contrast to Watteau's subtlety, an obvious one who reduced Watteau's transmutation of sexual byplay to the level of amorous anecdote. The best Pater only makes you wish for a real Watteau (see page 77).

Lancret (who, like Watteau, was trained under Gillot) followed Watteau's manner more closely but missed his spirit even more completely. He is often so explicitly an illustrator, as in the *Picnic after the Hunt* (page 76), that he earns for himself Jeurat's description of Watteau as a painter who marvelously imitated nature. "Painters after Nature" became the tag attached to any French artist of the time who worked in an informal manner as opposed to the "grand manner" that still ruled the Academy.

*A*ctually, the grand manner had become an anachronism with the death of Louis XIV, but Watteau had never been sufficiently conspicuous to threaten its conventional popularity. The break was made by François Boucher (1703–1770), who as an ambitious youngster had worked on the engravings of the *Recueil Julienne*. Watteau had been a private painter. Boucher was an aggressively public artist who came to rule the Academy as court painter to Mme de Pompadour and effected the perfect compromise between high society's public ambitions toward aesthetic learning and its private preoccupation with erotic stimulation. He rescaled the pomposities of the old style, bringing them into harmony with the feminine intimacy of the eighteenth-century drawing room.

Boucher's *Bath of Diana* (page 75) is sufficient demonstration of both his merits and his shortcomings. In many ways a delicious picture, it puts the goddess into the typical Boucher mold of a nubile grisette whose seductive, if slightly rubbery, pinkness is sweetly set off by moist lips and golden locks. Upon fresh, tiny-nippled breasts, jewels might lie as if upon a jeweler's cushion. A superb craftsman-designer with an infallible sense of decoration, Boucher did not think of paintings as independent statements (or as statements of any kind, apparently) but as part of a decorative ensemble. In his way he has never been surpassed. He became the Rubens of the boudoir, in boudoirs where Rubens would have seemed grossly overstated and out of scale.

We cannot call this a Watteau tradition; it is offered only as an example of the French world of elegance and cultivation that Watteau had poeticized, as it was interpreted at mid-century. The end of the sequence came with Jean Honoré Fragonard (1732–1806), a pupil of Boucher who is so appealing that he inspires absolutely unsupportable reveries—such as that he and Watteau would have got along beautifully if they had known one another; that Fragonard was what Watteau might have

been if he were a participant instead of an observer of the now decaying society. "Delightful" may be an adjective of minimum praise when it is employed to summarize a painter's work, indicating that his achievement is something less than impressive; in Fragonard's case, we can make it "consummately delightful" to give full credit to the most underrated artist of pre-Revolutionary France.

There must have been no young blade in Paris who enjoyed the city's special pleasures more than Fragonard did. Like Watteau, he found affluent patrons who were not only *bon vivants* but also eighteenth-century *amateurs* of the most cultivated type. He was tremendously successful, not only as a painter but also as a personality; his name was affectionately shortened to "Frago," and his conquests included some impressive names among the ladies of the demimonde.

Frago was as skilled a decorator as Boucher, and alone among eighteenth-century French painters of fashion had a sensitivity comparable in degree, although not in character, to Watteau's. There was nothing that Frago could not do, except what Watteau did: he could not rise above the society of gallant caprice in which he moved with such zest. If he had tried, he would likely have broken his bootstraps. But few artists are so complete within their boundaries as Fragonard is within his, and it is absurd to mistake these boundaries—which could include a painting like *The Swing* (opposite)—for the limitations of a minor talent. An art of consummate delight, after all, can be created only within boundaries that ignore most of the world.

Fragonard and Watteau drew their material from essentially the same society. But for Watteau, it was, as the English critic Walter Pater wrote in the nineteenth century, "that impossible or forbidden world which the mason's boy saw through the closed gateways of the enchanted garden."

This eighth in a series about great artists by John Canaday, art editor of The New York Times, *is adapted from one section of a forthcoming book by Mr. Canaday to be published by W. W. Norton & Co.*

For further reading: Watteau, Sa Vie—Son Oeuvre, *a biography in French, with extensive illustrations, by Hélène Adhémar and René Huyghe (Tisné, Paris, 1950);* Great Draughtsmen from Pisanello to Picasso, *with a discussion of thirty-seven illustrations of Watteau's drawings, by Jakob Rosenberg (Harvard University Press, 1959); for general reading,* French Painting *by R. H. Wilenski (Medici Society, London, revised 1949).*

"The bringer of food . . . creator of all good, lord

of majesty" is no longer worshiped as a god, but it still

controls the lives of the men who live along its banks

The Nile

By LORD KINROSS

Photographed for HORIZON
by ELIOT ELISOFON

The river Nile, stretching across half of Africa, flows northward from the tropical mountains and forests of the equator to the temperate Mediterranean Sea. It is the world's longest river, reaching 4,150 miles from the lakes that feed it and the streams that feed those lakes. Of Egypt, the land with which it is most closely associated and which the Nile fructifies for the last thousand miles of its course, Herodotus wrote that it is an acquired country, "the gift of the river." So it is. But the river itself is, in a sense, the gift of man. "Help yourself," runs an Egyptian proverb, "and the Nile will help you." The Nile as we see it today is the product of peoples who have been helping themselves for the past five thousand years. It is a supreme gift, not only of the equatorial rains, but of man with his inherent adaptability, industry, inventiveness, courage, curiosity, and sense of adventure.

The Greeks saw Egypt as an earthly paradise, a fit place, as they said, for the first generations of men. The Israelites, too, admired the richness of Egypt; wandering in the wilderness, they yearned for the land they had left, "when we sat by the fleshpots and when we did eat bread to the full"; they remembered the flesh and the fish and "the cucumbers, and the melons, and the leeks, and the onions, and the garlic." Both peoples were inclined to see such blessings as fruits of the bounty of nature, abundant since the beginning of time. In fact, Egypt was no such paradise until the Egyptians of prehistory started to make it so, subjugating a river whose flow was more wanton than bountiful.

During the millenniums preceding the dynastic history of Egypt, which begins around 3200 B.C., the ending of the Ice Age gradually dried up the grasslands which bordered the Nile, transforming the pastures of herdsmen and hunters into waterless desert. Yet the river itself remained, sprawling through this desert,

At Murchison Falls (opposite) near one of the sources of the Nile, the river tumbles down more than a hundred feet.
The relief above depicts the ancient Nile god, Hapi, a male deity with a woman's breasts, symbolizing fertility.

OPPOSITE: *Dozens of tropical mountain streams such as this one rise in the Ruwenzori range of western Uganda and flow toward Lake Albert, to provide water for one of the major sources of the Nile River.*

RIGHT: *A young Sudanese tribesman of the Sudd region wears a helmet made of cowdung and ashes to keep his coiffure in order.*

overflowing its banks into jungle swamps and water-logged marshes, where hippopotamuses and crocodiles flourished and vegetation ran rife and unproductive. A new, environmental challenge thus confronted the inhabitants of the valley and its neighboring lands. To this, it seems, they responded in two contrasting ways.

Some evaded the challenge, taking the line of least resistance. Their progeny survives among the Nilotic tribesmen of the Southern Sudan, primitive men living still in an environment of virgin nature. Here, in a tropical region perennially watered by rain, is a wilderness of swamps known as the Sudd, in which the river loses half its waters. Traversing a labyrinth of streams and inlets and lakes, its main channels have no fixed banks, but pass between floating masses of vegetable matter—"floes" of matted papyrus and reeds, forever shifting this way and that to block the river's course. Where a foothold exists in these sprawling, steaming marshes, naked African tribesmen, the Dinka and the Shilluk, have perched. "Gentle savages," long-legged like waterfowl, long-speared to hunt game, they live in primeval indolence, ruled by kings whom they believe have magical powers and worshiping the same totems and fetishes that the predynastic Egyptians did. Such still is life over much of the upper Nile valley.

Below the First Cataract near Aswan, where Egypt properly begins, it is different. Here other tribesmen made a more positive response to the challenge. They faced up to the change in their climate by changing their whole way of living. Stirring themselves to action, they drained the swamps and the marshes, canalized the river between dikes and diverted some of its flow into ditches and basins with low mud walls. Thus they reclaimed soil on which they grew their food instead of gathering it. Unlike their less spirited neighbors, they imposed themselves on their environment and thereby transformed Egypt into a cultivated land rich in cereals, vegetables, fodder, oil crops, and—in later times—sugar cane and cotton. Their descendants are the industrious fellahin, toiling in their millions throughout the lower Nile valley today.

The Nile valley was to develop into the Egyptian landscape so familiar to us now—a long ribbon of green cultivation which threads its way through the sun-bleached desert, vividly coloring the deep-soiled plain of Thebes; continuing seaward above ancient Memphis (now merely a palm grove across the river from Cairo), it broadens into a delta crisscrossed by irrigation channels to cover the black earth with a thick plaid of ordered and perennial fertility. 'Amr ibn-al-'As, the Arab who conquered the country in the seventh century A.D., poetically said of it: "Egypt is a dusty city and a green tree . . . The Nile traces a line through its midst; blessed are its early morning voyages and its travels at eventide. . . . At one season Egypt is a white pearl; then golden amber; then a green emerald; then an embroidery of many colors." Thus had man and the Nile, working jointly and in harmony, fashioned an agricultural "paradise."

This transformation of the Nile valley and of the lives of its people was gradual; it spread over hundreds, indeed, thousands of years. Portrayed on the walls of tombs of the Old Kingdom are thickets of reeds and papyrus where men hunt the hippopotamus, the crocodile, and other creatures of the swamp no longer to be seen north of the First Cataract. But as time went on, murals of peasant activities came to predominate—ploughing fields with teams of oxen, sowing seed, drawing water with the shaduf, an apparatus of buckets on poles that is still in use today, reaping and threshing crops, treading grapes to make wine.

The process of domestication, slow as it may have been, was continuous from before the third millennium, when the two kingdoms of Upper and Lower Egypt were drawn together into one united kingdom. This act of political union, so early in history, made possible the harnessing of the river and Egypt's subsequent economic development. It took a strong central authority to execute the major works of engineering required to control the great river (and incidentally to build the Pyramids as well), to mobilize labor and the other resources needed for the reclamation of land, and, above all, to maintain these works. For the annual Nile flood, on which the economy depended, was irregular, affording the narrowest margin of security. Fed by rainfall beyond Egypt's boundaries, no one knew exactly where, the river could be a foot too high one year, bursting its dikes to inundate villages and drown herds of cattle, and a foot too low the next, failing to rise sufficiently and thus creating drought and famine. Over the length of the Nile co-ordination was needed— to measure its level at certain times with Nilometers set up at various locations along its banks, to check and distribute and conserve its waters and thus ensure a supply which was reasonably constant.

All this called for a high degree of organization and planning, for scientific knowledge, clear practical thinking and technical skill. While other countries exerted their energies upon wars to determine their history, Egypt, flanked by desert barriers, was able to exert hers upon the river, and her history was determined accordingly. Hers was essentially a fluvial society. Only at periods when the country was under a strong government was Egypt economically secure. At other periods, under the pressure of internal dissension or occasional external invasion, it disintegrated easily—and the river was likely to take over from man.

Napoleon was perspicacious enough, in his brief occupation of Egypt in A.D. 1798, to pronounce it a country easy to govern. "There is no country in the world," he wrote, "where the government controls more closely, by means of the Nile, the life of the people. Under a good administration the Nile gains on the desert; under a bad one, the desert gains on the Nile." So it was that dynasty after dynasty of Pharaohs controlled the lives of the Egyptian people, with varying effectiveness, over a period of three thousand years, from the fourth millennium until the Romans conquered Egypt in 30 B.C.

The rule of the Pharaohs was autocratic, but it did not necessarily seem tyrannical to their subjects. For the Egyptians, during the good periods, enjoyed the security of the fruits of the Nile and of permanent employment. During the months of the flood, when no work could be done in the fields, they would be recruited to build pyramids, tombs, and temples for their masters. Work was always available and, like the fellahin of today, the ancient Egyptians were by nature a hard-working people. Moreover, submission to authority was inherent in their religious beliefs. The Pharaohs clinched their political and economic hold over the lower Nile valley by the assumption of godhead. To his subjects, each Pharaoh was a god as well as an earthly ruler.

The land of Egypt was the gift not only of the Nile but of the Sun, which was visible from morning until evening in a cloud-free, mist-free sky. The slow, undeviating cycle of the sun was Egypt's life-beat, setting the rhythm of every man's day. Thus the Egyptian worshiped, above all other deities, the sun-god—and was not the Pharaoh, by miraculous conception, "the son of his belly," "the one whom he had begotten," and thus God in his own right? All that invested and surrounded the Pharaoh was sacred. The crowns he wore on his head, the sceptre he bore, even his beard, were symbols of the supernatural, endowed in themselves with divine power. Each morning the Pharaoh performed ritual ablutions like those which the sun-god supposedly made in the waters of heaven, thus equipping himself to dispense heavenly grace to his subjects, for whom the life of the day would not otherwise be thought to have begun. Approaching him, Egyptians assumed a posture of worship, "smelling the earth, crawling the ground, invoking this Perfect God and exalting his beauty." When he died, he "flew away up to heaven and was united with the Sun— and his divine limbs were absorbed into Him who created him"; and throughout the afterlife he sailed through the firmament in the company of his father, the Sun.

Hardly less important to the Egyptian people than the sun-god was Hapi, the spirit of the Nile. The annual Nile flood was the "arrival of Hapi," who was often depicted in colors of green and blue, like the waters before the inundation, and as long-haired and naked like a fisherman in the swamps. Hymns were sung to this god "who nourishes, feeds, and finds provender for the whole of Egypt. . . . abundance being in his path, nourishment at his fingertips and whose coming brings joy to every human being . . . Thou art unique; on the day when thou goest forth from the cavern everyone rejoices. Thou art the master of the fish and thou art rich in wheat-fields." A rapturous worshiper would sing, "Thou art verdant, thou art verdant, O Nile." The Nile was the measure of all greatness, so that one Pharaoh could exclaim, "May men one day say of me, he was a Nile." This was a sentiment echoed —albeit in reverse—some thousands of years later by Amr, who accorded the river the dignity of a caliph.

Each year at flood time the divinity of the river was propitiated by offerings, the priests flinging gold and precious gifts into its waters, and the people adding amulets, cakes, fruits, sacrificial animals, and female figurines to stimulate fertility. The annual ceremony of cutting the dikes to let the flood waters through was accompanied by festivities, as it still is in the city of Cairo today.

But there were other gods, too, in profusion. The ancient Egyptians were a people who saw magic in everything around them. They sensed the divine spirit in every creature, whether human or animal. Thus the familiar birds and beasts of the Nile valley, often endowed with human bodies and princely regalia, played a prominent role in their system of worship. The sky-goddess, for example, had the head of a cow, the sky-god, Horus, the head of a falcon, the moon-god, that of an ibis. In later times other animals—dogs, cats, and especially bulls—were regarded as sacred, and mummified after death. As the centuries passed, the deity who came to be most loved and revered by the Egyptian masses was Osiris. Born of the god of the Earth and the goddess of the Sky, he went through the cycle of death and resurrection, like the Phoenician god Adonis and like Christ in the Christian story, becoming the symbol not merely of vegetable life in its death and renewal with the passage of the seasons but of spiritual life as well.

Osiris in human form was believed to have been the first to introduce the cultivation of grain into the Nile valley, to take fruit from the trees, to train vines to poles, and tread the grapes for wine. The harvesting of the crops came to represent his martyrdom at the hands of his brother Set, the symbol of drought and sterility; at the harvest, Osiris's body was severed, as it were, by the sickle of the reaper, and trampled by cattle on the threshing floor. The annual rising of the Nile was considered the flood of the tears of his bereaved wife, the goddess Isis. When the flood subsided and the seed was sown again, his body was believed to have fertilized the new crop.

Meanwhile Osiris reigned over the underworld as King of the Dead, opening the gates of eternal life—at first, during the earlier period, only to a privileged and powerful few, but later, in a democratic and moral spirit, to all who could prove themselves innocent of specified sins.

The ancient Egyptians knew no other world but their long river valley, a secure "oasis" walled in between the broad desert wastes which only occasional raiding Bedouin tribes would venture to cross. The world beyond it meant little to them. For the first fifteen hundred years of their recorded history, they suffered no foreign invasion and attempted no foreign expansion. The source of the Nile was unknown to them beyond the fact that it was located in an unfamiliar "Land of Ghosts and Spirits" somewhere to the south. At first the river was believed to gush forth from the underworld through a mythical

The fresco above, a representation of the heavens from the ceiling of Ramses VI's tomb at Thebes, contains a double portrait of the sky-goddess Nut arched above the earth. Another Nile, a mythical river in the sky, along which the Egyptians believed the sun sailed each day until it was swallowed at nightfall by the sky-goddess, can be seen as a broad ribbon flowing toward Nut's mouth. All night the sun's barge was towed along the river by star-gods, and in the morning Nut gave birth to it again. The course of the earthly Nile, long though it is, is not quite so complex. The map at left shows the river from its source in Lake Victoria to its mouth at the Mediterranean.

cavern of Hapi, above the First Cataract. But early in the third millennium a military expedition into Nubia, beyond the First Cataract, showed that the river originated in remoter African lands many hundreds of miles to the south.

Thereafter the southern frontier of Egypt was extended, little by little, upstream to the Second Cataract and the Third. Expeditions to these and the neighboring regions would return laden with such treasures as incense, ivory, ebony, panther skins, and Negro slaves—and once with a dancing pygmy as a gift for a boy Pharaoh. As time went on, the savage Nubians came to be a potential threat to Egyptian security. Fortresses were built in the south, and a wall was constructed along the river for the protection of shipping; finally a boundary stone was set up near the present town of Wadi Halfa, "in order to forbid any Negro to pass it by water or by land, either with a ship or with any herds of cattle, forever." At no time did the ancient Egyptians penetrate farther south than the present-day city of Khartoum in the Sudan. Herodotus, who traveled only as far as the First Cataract, could not obtain any information about the source of the river beyond the report that it arose from "fountains" somewhere in the center of Africa.

In Roman times Nero sent two centurions and a body of men through the Sudan to search for the source of the Nile. But they returned with the report that their way had been blocked by an impenetrable swamp in the interior—the Sudd. A little later a Greek merchant, traveling inland from the East African coast, came upon two great lakes and a snow-capped range and declared that this was the source of the river. It was depicted as such on a map by the Greek geographer Ptolemy, who called the range the "Mountains of the Moon." Otherwise, Homer's description of the Nile as "heaven-descended" was to stand until the nineteenth century—when it was found to approximate, in a sense, the truth.

For it was not until the nineteenth century that the source of the Nile was finally discovered. As the lower Nile had presented a challenge to the people of Egypt five thousand years earlier, so now did the upper Nile—in its two branches, the White and the Blue—come to present a challenge, of a different sort, to the thrusting peoples of the Western world. It had first been taken up toward the end of the eighteenth century by the stalwart son of an old Scottish family, James Bruce, who in an arduous journey found the source of the Blue Nile. Pouring out of Lake Tana, in the Ethiopian highlands, it passes over a series of cataracts and rapids to join the main stream of the river, the White Nile, at Khartoum. From here these waters run distinct for a while, side by side in the same bed, more gray and green than white and blue; they finally merge, and, fed by only one more stream, the Atbara, flow unbroken for sixteen hundred miles to the Medi-

terranean. The Blue Nile is indeed descended from the skies as Homer says—from rain borne over equatorial jungles by southwesterly winds from the Atlantic, which breaks each spring against the volcanic peaks of Ethiopia, dissolving metallic matter and, at flood time, depositing over Egypt the river's life-giving alluvium of silt.

Despite the discovery of the Blue Nile's source, the source of the White Nile remained a blank space on the African map. By the mid-nineteenth century most of the world had been traversed and mapped. The time had come to solve this geographical mystery, which the ancient Egyptians and the Romans had failed to do, and which their successors along the Nile, the Arabs and Turks, had barely tackled. Here was a quest that appealed to the imagination of this inquiring and adventurous age of discovery. The curiosity of the explorer was reinforced by a missionary spirit bent on preaching the Gospel to the heathen savages of Africa and on abolishing the slave trade to which they were subjected; by commercial enterprise concerned with profits derived from trade in ivory and such precious minerals as Central Africa might afford; and finally by competition among the rival European powers for political influence, for the flag followed exploration and trade. Among the British especially, now in their heyday of imperialist expansion, there arose a Victorian breed of tough and eccentric explorers who sought an outlet for their peculiar energies that was denied them at home. Thus Burton, Speke, Baker, Grant, Livingstone, Stanley, and Gordon, together with such foreign contestants as the German Emin, the Italian Romolo Gessi, and the Frenchman Jean-Baptiste Marchand, made their successive contributions to the opening up of a dark continent and to the discovery of the course of the world's most remarkable river.

First in the field were Richard Burton and John Speke. Each was in his thirties, and a former officer in the Indian army; otherwise they were men of a very different stamp —Burton the romantic Orientalist, the scholar, the eccentric, the rake; Speke the practical, prudent Victorian, abstemious, quietly determined, and dedicated to the healthy life of the soldier. Traveling inland together from Zanzibar in 1857, through country where no white man had previously trod, they sought the great lakes and mountains from which the Nile must flow. They soon disagreed. Reaching Lake Tanganyika, which Burton had persuaded himself was the source of the river, they found, not the Nile, but only the report of a stream running southward. Speke then proceeded northward alone, attracted by word of another, larger lake. This he discovered and named Lake Victoria in honor of his sovereign, claiming with intuitive conviction that it was the source of the Nile. Burton ridiculed this unscientific conclusion, insisting, no more scientifically, that the "Mountains of the Moon" lay between Speke's lake and the Nile.

Speke's discovery, nonetheless, so impressed the Royal Geographical Society in London that it financed another expedition, in which Burton was offered no part. This time Speke went to Africa in the company of Captain James Grant, another Indian army officer and a man who was modestly content to serve as Speke's lieutenant. They traveled together, setting out for the northern shores of Lake Victoria. Here, as it chanced, it was Speke alone who reached the Nile and discovered the point at which it emerged from the lake, pouring itself over a mighty waterfall which he named Ripon Falls after the president of the Royal Geographical Society who had helped to further the expedition. Thence, rejoined by Grant, he proceeded northward, largely overland, following the direction of the river until, at an Egyptian fort and trading post at Gondokoro, opposite the present post of Juba, they encountered, in Speke's words, "the form of an Englishman . . . my old friend Baker, famed for his sports in Ceylon," who had come upstream from Khartoum in search of him.

Speke maintained that Lake Victoria was a source of the Nile, whatever Burton might say. But was there a possible second source that flowed from a second lake to the west of Victoria? After meeting the two explorers and seeing them off down the river to Cairo, Samuel Baker, a stalwart man whose appetite for exploration was stimulated by a love of big-game shooting, continued to travel upstream to find out, accompanied by his resolute wife. At the end of an interminable journey fraught with every misadventure, they found "that great reservoir of Nature that ever since creation had baffled discovery" and, after drinking from it deeply, named it Lake Albert for the Prince Consort, who had lately died. They found finally the point at which the river entered the lake, flowing through a ravine to thunder down from a great height in a narrow, dramatic cascade. This they named Murchison Falls after another president of the Royal Geographical Society.

Still there was no final proof that either or both of the two streams flowing out of the two lakes were the ultimate sources of the Nile. Indeed, Baker's discovery of Lake Albert only encouraged Burton and other detractors of Speke in their theory that the Nile might originate in another river to the south of it—even, as Burton had always claimed, from Lake Tanganyika. Doctor Livingstone, the great missionary and veteran of African explorations, inclined to such a theory, believing, as Herodotus had hinted, that the river sprang from deep fountains at the foot of a great mountain range. He was thus

TEXT CONTINUED ON PAGE 97

In Upper Egypt two peasants equipped with a net wade through the Nile-flooded fields searching for fish from the river

Birds and Beasts

A Roman painting from Pompeii (right) shows the pygmies of the upper Nile hunting the fearsome beasts that abounded along the river. One dwarf, less fortunate than his fellows, is about to be decapitated by a hippopotamus. The Romans were intrigued by the exotic landscape of the Nile and depicted it often in mosaics and paintings. Opposite, crocodiles and a hippopotamus are seen basking in the sun along the banks of the Victoria Nile in the country of Uganda.

The Nile valley lies along one of the world's great flyways, over which northern birds migrate annually to spend the winter in Africa. Egypt is astonishingly rich in bird life, as a glance at any hieroglyphic text will show, for many syllables are represented by birds. Birds are still common, but the great beasts of antiquity—notably crocodiles and hippopotamuses—have disappeared from Egypt. Farther south, the crocodile is endangered by indiscriminate hunting, and the hippopotamus is far less common than it was before the Europeans came. Both beasts were feared by the ancient Egyptians, as they are by the Nile tribesmen of today. The crocodile was described as "the raging one who seizes powerfully, and if he seizes, there is no one who can be freed." The hippopotamus became a symbol of the world's evil, for a nocturnal visit from a hippo, which can devour fifty pounds of grass in a night and trample much more than that, could destroy the farmwork of an entire season.

In ancient Egypt, only aristocrats, like the man shown in the wall painting opposite, were permitted to hunt waterfowl with a throwstick; it was one of their favorite diversions. They sailed through the swamps in skiffs made of papyrus reeds, accompanied by pet cats trained to retrieve game. Above, a flock of migratory birds stand in a field that has been flooded by the slowly rising waters of the Nile.

In a wall painting from Pharaonic times (right) the shaduf is being employed to water a rich man's garden. Opposite, peasants work the same device to raise river water up to the fields along the Nile's banks in Upper Egypt. In some places where the banks are high, two or three shadufs are used in series in order to lift the water to the required height.

The River's Bounty

The mud of the Nile is so famous for its fertility that Egyptian women sometimes eat lumps of it scooped from the river bottom to make sure they will be fertile themselves. Its effect on them has never been measured (although Egypt does have one of the world's highest birth rates); but its effect on the land which the river floods is considerable. In some places along the Nile, fields can produce three crops a year. In the past century and a half, since the time when the pasha Mohammed Ali began to modernize the country, a more effective method of irrigation has been one of the government's major concerns; new dams and canals have brought a regular supply of Nile water to many farms whose peasants had traditionally depended on bringing water to their land by hand. But the ancient water-raising methods are still used. Throughout Egypt one can still see men watering their fields with the shaduf, a bucket raised by hand, and the sakieh, a water wheel that is worked by animal power.

90

The fellah, or peasant, directly below is threshing grain. The wall painting below, opposite, which dates from the fifteenth century B.C., shows in a detail two farm workers preparing a threshing floor by spreading out the wheat with pitchforks similar to those in use today.

From Pharaoh to Farouk

Moses and Pharaoh's daughter

The mummy of Ramses II (1292–1225 B.C.)

Cleopatra (69–30 B.C.)

A lady of the third century

Mohammed Ali (1769–1849)

Ancient Egyptians rejoiced in the thought that their country was without history. Their view of the world was static: the best life was one in which everything was always the same. The Nile rose, flooded, and receded; the sun crossed the sky; the Pharaoh, no matter who he was, was always considered the son of the sun-god. This feeling of continuity was so strong that many Pharaohs gave the names of old conquests to new cities they conquered, and one named his children, dogs, and pet lion after the children, dogs, and pet lion of a predecessor.

As any modern Egyptian schoolboy or army conscript can testify, Egypt is no longer so fortunate. It has been burdened with more history than almost any other nation and is still, of course, being subjected to it. The heritage of Nasser's Egypt includes far more than the thirteen-century Arab experience of which the official propagandists boast so proudly. Egypt also means Cleopatra, a well-known Grecian lady (her forebears were Macedonian) who sailed down the Nile in her splendid barge, and the Hebrew emancipator, Moses, who was saved by Pharaoh's daughter from drowning in that same river. It means, too, the men who conquered the Nile valley—Alexander the Great and Augustus, the great Arab generals and the Ottoman Turks, and Napoleon Bonaparte.

Jesus belongs here almost as much as Mohammed does. He, after all, was taken to the country as an infant. A few centuries later, His followers even took over Egypt and consigned the ancient gods of the country to the Land of the Dead. In Alexandria scholars argued and defined His intimate and complex relationship with God, His Father, and the Holy Ghost. And in the Upper Egyptian desert, near the city of Thebes, Christian monasticism had its beginnings. When the Arabs conquered the country in A.D. 640, the Christian inhabitants of Egypt were offered toleration. But by the ninth century, when the last Christian rebellion against Arab rule took place, they had become a minority; time and the attraction of belonging to a powerful majority had been enough to cause a great decrease in their numbers. Their conversion to Islam had a profound effect on the country's economy, for Christians were taxed more heavily than Moslems. Despite this loss in revenue, Egypt changed inexorably into an Arab nation, although only a small percentage of the population was of Arab blood. Today Egypt's Christians, or Copts, are a small and powerless group, but they are the only inhabitants who can claim a direct link with Pharaonic times; their religious liturgy preserves the language of ancient Egypt, and their script is derived, although distantly, from the hieroglyphs of antiquity.

For several centuries after the Arab conquest, under the caliphs who ruled the new Islamic domains from their capital at Baghdad, Egypt was a province of a far larger empire. But late in the ninth century the Nile valley became independent again, under a dynasty called the

e murder of Tūrān-Shah (1250)

A Mamlūk

British caricature of Napoleon's flight from Egypt in 1799

modern Nubian

The explorer Belzoni (1778–1823)

Tulunids. In the centuries that followed, Egypt once more developed an independent culture, and its capital, Cairo, grew into the metropolis of Islam. In the year 988 the academy which was to evolve into the greatest university in the Moslem world was founded in the city. By the eleventh century, Cairo was famous for its wealth, its learning, and the beauty of its mosques. "He who has not seen Cairo," wrote the famous medieval Arab scholar ibn-Khaldūn, "does not know the grandeur of Islam."

That grandeur was challenged by the Crusaders, whose arrival in the Middle East affected Egypt profoundly. It was the Crusades that gave Egypt one of its greatest rulers, Saladin, who gained his throne and established his dynasty by his skill in fighting what modern Egyptians might call a Western imperialist colonial incursion into Arab territory. Among the "Western imperialist adventurers" who visited Egypt during the Crusades were two saints, Francis of Assisi, and Louis King of France. Francis came to preach Christianity to one of Saladin's successors, the amiable and tolerant sultan al-Kāmil. A few years and sultans later, Louis invaded the country and was taken prisoner with some of his men. As a captive, he was on hand to witness the unhappy end of Saladin's dynasty, when Tūran-Shāh, the last of the line, was killed by his stepmother's slaves in the river Nile.

For more than a century thereafter, Egypt was ruled by a coterie called the Mamlūks, recruited from palace slaves. Under their government, sultans changed with astonishing rapidity, but the country itself prospered, for it controlled the trade routes between Europe and the East. With Baghdad destroyed by the Mongols, and the Moslem cities of Spain overrun by the Christians, Cairo dominated the Moslem world. But after the fifteenth century, when Western explorers found alternate routes for trading with India, a deadening economic depression overcame Egypt.

The Ottoman Turks conquered the country in 1517. As a distant province of a corrupt ill-governed empire, Egypt sank into centuries of decadence, from which it was awakened only at the end of the eighteenth century when Napoleon invaded the country to block the British route to India. After him came scholars and explorers, such as the Italian Giovanni Belzoni. The antiquities were studied, the hieroglyphics deciphered, and expeditions sent out to discover the source of the Nile. In 1811 Mohammed Ali, a soldier in the Turkish army, seized control of the country and, like an enlightened eighteenth-century despot, proceeded to modernize it. But the pace of modernization was slow, for his descendants, down to the late King Farouk, were less competent or less benevolent than he had been. They borrowed money so recklessly that the country was soon in pawn—with the English as pawnbrokers—a situation which prevailed until the last British troops withdrew from Egypt in 1952.

93

During a part of each year the waters of the Nile submerge the temple of Isis on the island of Philae near Aswan. The Egyptian government

Rescuing the Past

lanning to build a retaining dam which will protect the temple from the rising waters of the river and keep it dry all seasons of the year

When the Aswan Dam is completed, a three-hundred-mile stretch of the river behind it will be transformed into a lake to be named after President Nasser. This impressive monument to the accomplishments of Egypt's present ruler will drown the works of many of his predecessors. The sites of about a dozen temples will be flooded, but most of the buildings themselves are being saved. Ramses II's temple of Abu Simbel is being cut into blocks and raised bit by bit to a new site, two hundred feet above the new level of the river. There it will be reassembled, a splendid engineering feat in a land that has seen many engineering marvels. Several other, smaller temples are also being cut into blocks, and offered to foreign nations which have given Egypt help in saving Abu Simbel. One of them, Dendur, is coming to America, where a number of cities are competing for the right to give it a home.

The temple of Abu Simbel (opposite) is being carved into neat pieces for lifting to the new site. Three faces of Pharaoh Ramses II are seen at right, waiting patiently for the crane. Below them are his beards and bodies, which have been covered with sand for their temporary protection.

TEXT CONTINUED FROM PAGE 87

ready to accept Murchison's invitation on behalf of the Society to return to Africa and finally settle the problem.

Ironically it was not Livingstone who settled it, for his travels took him on a false track far off course to the south. Instead it was the man who, after Livingstone had been lost to the world for four years, was sent out as a newspaper correspondent to search for him. This was Henry Morton Stanley, a go-getting, tough, practical adventurer who had grown up in a Welsh workhouse, emigrated to America, and taken up journalism as a means of making his fortune and his name as an explorer. Stanley found Livingstone, who was to die in Africa soon after their famous encounter. Then, in a series of journeys, he sailed around Lake Victoria, proving it to be a single lake with a single outlet to the Nile; he sailed around Lake Tanganyika, proving it to have no outlet to the Nile; he sailed down the neighboring Lualaba river, which Livingstone had thought to be a source of the Nile, and found it to be a source of the Congo. In a later journey he finally located the "Mountains of the Moon," the peaks of the Ruwenzori range, whose "heaven-descended" snows drain into Lake Albert and thence into the Nile. Meanwhile the course of the Nile southward from Gondokoro to Lake Albert had finally been traced. This was done partly in a second journey by Baker, in which he forced a passage through the Sudd after months of obstruction, but largely by Gordon, who, in the service of the Khedive of Egypt, opened up most of the river to navigation before he was killed by fanatical Moslem rebels in Khartoum.

Thus the blank space on the map of Africa was filled; no longer was there a "land of ghosts" beyond the First Cataract; European man had met the ultimate challenge of the Nile, completing the work of Egyptian man in the earliest days of his history. The lives of the people on the upper Nile now changed. Eventually they were freed from the tyranny of the slave trade. For many, Christianity and Islam, often in conflict, came to replace primitive tribal beliefs. Modern administration imposed order upon them. Modern cultivation followed it. The British flag—flying side by side with the Egyptian as far as the Southern Sudan—brought them a form of political unity. Above all it unified the river itself, and this unity has to some extent survived its subsequent disappearance.

British administration led to the co-ordinated construction of dams and barrages throughout the length of the Nile, from the great lakes to points close to the river's two mouths at Rosetta and Damietta. This control of the waters was designed to replace the old system of basin irrigation by one of perennial irrigation. The conversion was accomplished in an area that covered five-sixths of the cultivated land of Egypt, permitting the growth of two or more crops each year instead of one, as before,

Near Luxor a carefully planned network of canals brings the river's inundation to fields at the very edge of the desert.

and facilitating the production of cotton, which needs water at a season when the river is naturally low. The old Aswan Dam—completed by the British in 1902 and heightened twice since then—conserves water in the flood season and releases it as the flow abates, thus affording an even supply. Thanks to this, the lower Nile valley is today the most intensively cultivated agricultural area in the world.

But it is also one of the most densely populated areas in the world. With births occurring at the rate of a child a minute, the fertility of the Egyptian people outruns that of their land. Thus, a century after the discovery of the river's sources, another challenge awaits man in the valley of the Nile. It is being met by the construction of a new High Dam a few miles upstream from the old dam at Aswan. "A mountain of a dam," as an Egyptian described it; two miles across, rising 350 feet from the river bed, it is to contain behind its great walls one of the world's largest reservoirs, to be known as Lake Nasser. It will submerge a large part of Nubia, depriving residents of their riverside villages (which are already evacuated), and obliging them to settle elsewhere. On the site, the lake will store the equivalent of a whole year's floodwaters.

This will make Egypt independent of the vagaries of the annual inundation, which may provide either disastrously more or disastrously less than the country needs; independent, too, of human and political caprices beyond its borders, of threats of interference with the supply by other powers on the banks of the Nile farther south. It will enable Egypt to cultivate one million more acres of land—almost double the total cultivated at present—and to convert an additional million from basin to perennial irrigation, thus adding two million acres to the six million now cultivated. It will provide hydroelectric power for the development of industry, thereby offering alternative employment to an expanding population and raising the general standard of living. Appropriately, beside this mighty modern Egyptian monument, President Nasser has placed a statue of the Pharoah who, four thousand years ago, similarly contained and controlled a lake in the oasis of the Fayum and in effect became the father of the reservoir system of the Nile.

Thus if Egypt is still, as in the days of Herodotus, essentially an acquired country, "the gift of the river," it is a country more than ever acquired by man, through his progressive subjugation of its waters. The Nile valley is in truth a gift to civilization by the people of Egypt themselves.

Lord Kinross, who served for a number of years as First Secretary at the British embassy in Cairo, has written extensively about the Middle East. His most recent book is Atatürk, *a biography of the founder of modern Turkey.*

A water buffalo stands in a flooded field before the time-worn pyramids of Dahshûr, among the earliest to be built.

Reflections
on the
Curtain
Wall

Photographed for Horizon by Robert Stoller

In New York, most self-conscious of cities, even the buildings take
the measure of one another. Each towering new crystal palace
with its enveloping glass shell provides yet another shimmering screen
on which the light, the action, the color of the razzle-dazzle
cityscape is played. Sometimes the images are surrealistic—buildings
emerge from within buildings, automobiles seem to race along
window ledges at the fourteenth floor, neon lights intrude on corporate
symbols—and sometimes they are merely glittering patterns. In
these four pages photographer Robert Stoller offers a glimpse of the
continuous magic-lantern show that goes on above street (and
eye) level in any city where the smooth glass curtain-wall has taken over.

Like mirrors in a Fun House, the slightest ripple in these taut glass membranes can turn their subjects into strange and wonderful constructions. A neo-Gothic tower (the General Electric Building, left) casts its gaudy imprint on windows three blocks away; at the same time, a montage of anonymous brick and steel charts an irregular course on another graph-paper curtain wall (right).

Some twenty stories
above midtown Fifth Avenue,
an office building of the
'20's with Renaissance aspirations
preens her copper-clad
turrets in one facet of Corn-
ing's four and a half
acres of green-tinted glass-
works. The slender
steel mullions of the new
seem barely able to
contain the baroque ex-
uberance of the old,
a test of strength that adds
dimension to both of
these stylistic adversaries.

A Few Words
from the Etruscans

The Etruscans left no history of their own; Roman accounts were biased.

However, three inscribed gold tablets, recently discovered,

provide a new key to the long struggle for power in the ancient world, to the

decline of the Etruscans, and to the rise of an independent Rome

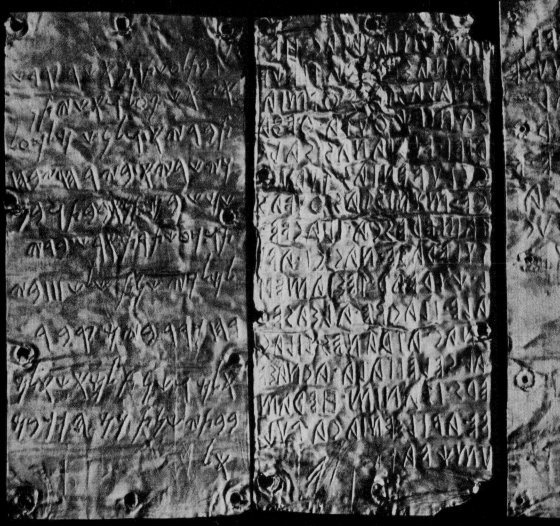

The three gold tablets above, recently found at Pyrgi near Rome, record in two languages the dedication of an Etruscan temple about 500 B.C. The tablet at left is written in Punic, the other two in Etruscan (for a translation, see page 106).

By M. I. FINLEY

ome produced no Homer. This is another way of saying that the Romans, unlike the Greeks and many other peoples, lacked the tradition—transmitted orally by bards for many centuries—that once upon a time there had been an age of heroes who performed deeds of valor against foes of equal caliber. This is the theme of the *Iliad* and the *Odyssey*, as of the Anglo-Saxon *Beowulf* and the French *Song of Roland*. Virgil's *Aeneid* is something very different, the work of a highly sophisticated poet writing with a considerable literary experience behind him (more like Dante or Milton than like the usually anonymous heroic poets), and writing specifically to fill the gap that the Romans, by then thoroughly imbued with Greek literature and Greek traditions, had become only too conscious of.

Heroes fight heroes—that is a pretty universal law. Homer's Trojans are indistinguishable from his Greeks, except that they are destined to defeat. But if one asks about Rome's greatest enemies in its formative and later in its conquering years, a very different picture emerges—as in Livy's *History*, written about five hundred years after Rome broke free from the Etruscans and two hundred years after they defeated the Carthaginians under Hannibal. Both the Etruscans and the Carthaginians had effectively disappeared as peoples by Livy's time. Whatever may have survived of their language, their religion, or their institutions had been woven into the language, religion, and institutions of Romanized Italy and North Africa. Thus, there were a few Etruscan words in Latin and a larger proportion of Etruscan rites and practices embedded in the religion of Italy, but only an occasional Roman antiquarian bothered to (or was able to) identify them as Etruscan elements, and then not always with any accuracy. And such literature of their own as may have existed has been sunk with hardly a trace. All we have, in its stead, is the Roman image of their enemies (plus some Greek elaboration)—nasty, brutish, mean, faithless, licentious. Here and there an individual stands out as something of an exception: Hannibal comes to mind, or the fictitious Dido, Virgil's queen of Carthage. But there are no Etruscan Hectors, no Carthaginian Priams.

It was not so very long ago that this victor's account of the vanquished was still accepted without a second thought. Then came a dramatic shift with respect to the Etruscans (but not the Carthaginians). "Antiquarian research, partaking of the quickened energy of the nineteenth century," led to the discovery of the Etruscan burial sites of central Italy, with their unparalleled artistic treasures. The words I have just quoted open George Dennis's *Cities and Cemeteries of Etruria*, the book that contributed more than any other in the English-speaking world to a new, highly romantic image of the Etruscans which ultimately found its climax in the blood mystique of D. H. Lawrence's *Etruscan Places*. Dennis belongs to that almost legendary group of amateur English explorers and archaeologists who, within a few decades, made the Western world aware of the buried and forgotten past of three continents.* His two volumes appeared in 1848, the fruits of five years of the most careful and systematic study of the sites and of anything there was to be read on the subject in his day. The work became a best seller.

*For another of the group, Robert Pashley, see HORIZON for Summer, 1965, 67-68.

To read George Dennis now is an exciting experience—and a sobering one: admiration for his energy, boldness, and intelligence is tempered by a realization that he (and his contemporaries) got the *history* hopelessly wrong. He (and they) could neither work out the chronological sequence of the archaeological evidence nor penetrate the distortions of the ancient traditions as reported by writers five hundred or more years after the event. He was most wrong in his predictions. The "internal history" of the Etruscans, he wrote, "promises, ere long, to be as distinct and palpable as that of Egypt, Greece, or Rome." More than a century has gone by, and that prediction has not been fulfilled. The reason is perfectly simple: as much as our knowledge of the Etruscans has grown and been corrected since Dennis wrote, it still rests almost entirely on material remains, and, worse still, on remains from tombs and cemeteries almost to the exclusion of anything else. One does one's best to interpret the Etruscan passion for Greek ceramics and for lions, or the enigmatic Etruscan "smile," or the life-sized sculptures of fat gentlemen reclining on the lids of their sarcophagi. But one cannot be reminded too often of what the late Llewellyn Brown said in his splendid book *The Etruscan Lion*: "Throughout this period . . . Etruscan artists were working in highly formalized traditions in which the essential features of the subjects portrayed were reduced to conventional formulae or stylizations, often of pattern-like quality."

If the interpretation of artistic conventions is to be anything more than the free play of the interpreter's imagination, he must have a key, which can be provided only by contemporary writing. And there lies the whole trouble. Not, as is widely believed, because the Etruscan alphabet (taken from the Greek) remains an unlocked secret, but because all but a handful of the more than ten thousand available texts are brief formulas, such as "Vel Partunu, son of Velthur and of Ramtha Satlnei, died aged twenty-eight", and also because no longish bilingual text turned up (comparable, for example, to the Rosetta stone, which gave Champollion the key to Egyptian hieroglyphics).

A break finally came in July, 1964. It was not the hoped-for document in Etruscan and Latin that the excavators found, but three separate overlapping tablets, two in Etruscan and the third in Punic, the Carthaginian dialect of old Phoenician—in sum, not only the first bilingual text (though not a true one, strictly speaking), but also the first Punic text from Etruria and just about the oldest Punic text ever found anywhere. It is too soon to say how much these will add to our knowledge of the Etruscan language, but they throw unexpected light on a vital phase of Etruscan history and also on ancient traditions concerning the founding of Rome.

The place of discovery was a little bathing resort on the Tyrrhenian Sea some thirty miles west by north of Rome, called Santa Severa. On a rock foundation jutting out over the sea stands a masonry wall built by the Romans in the third century B.C., and within the walled rectangle, a medieval castle. Nothing that one can see seems to merit any particular attention, but Professor Massimo Pallottino, the outstanding Etruscologist, decided to organize systematic excavation there in 1957 (under the direction of his pupil, Dr. Giovanni Colonna) because of an old, fragmentary, and tantalizing tradition about the place. Dennis already knew that Santa Severa was called in antiquity by the Greek name of Pyrgi. Virgil lists Pyrgi in his catalogue of Etruscan places, and his contemporary, the Greek geographer Strabo, adds that it had been the harbor for the Etruscan town of Agylla and that it has a temple of Eileithyia, built by the "Pelasgians," which used to be rich.

Strabo's shift of tenses is intentional: the temple was still standing in his day, but it was no longer important. If the god or goddess was in high repute, an ancient temple was often a storehouse of treasure; both states and individuals regularly made valuable dedications, notably tithes of booty captured in a war or raid. But a rich temple of Eileithyia is rather surprising anywhere, and especially in this region. Eileithyia was an ancient Greek deity, going back to Mycenaean and possibly even to Minoan times, who was particularly associated with childbirth and sometimes assimilated to Artemis, the Diana of the Romans. As for the "Pelasgians," that was just the commonest Greek label for the various indigenous peoples of the eastern Mediterranean, about whom they had only the foggiest—and largely inaccurate—notions. Strabo implies that Eileithyia's wealth at Pyrgi had been stolen long ago by Dionysius I, tyrant of Syracuse, an incident about which we have a slightly longer account from the Sicilian Greek historian Diodorus, who lived a generation or two before Strabo. According to Diodorus, in the year 384 B.C. Dionysius was planning yet another war with Carthage but lacked funds. On the pretext of wishing to clear the Tyrrhenian Sea of pirates, he came to Pyrgi and looted it, then devastated the territory of Agylla and took many captives, whom he sold as slaves. All told, that incursion brought him the vast sum of fifteen hundred talents, more than enough to hire and equip a large army.

That is about all, but it is enough to include most of the peoples who made up the history of this area down to and beyond the time of Dionysius—"Pelasgians" (whoever they may have been), Greeks, Etruscans, Carthaginians. Only the Romans are missing; properly so, since their role as a great power lay in the future. For several centuries southern Italy and Sicily had been the meeting point of peoples coming from different directions for different purposes, fighting or raiding at one moment, having peaceful intercourse at another, trading, intermarrying, exchanging ideas, amalgamating gods. Agylla was called Cisra by the Etruscans and Caere by the Romans. (Today it is Cerveteri.) It is not known what the Etruscan name for Pyrgi was, nor how and when the harbor town came to house the rather curious Greek goddess chosen. There is nothing surprising about the presence of a Greek goddess as such; the importation of foreign deities and their assimilation with native gods and goddesses was an unending process in antiquity, inevitable in a polytheistic world filled with contending and clashing peoples.

Now what the excavators of Pyrgi have found so far—and most of the site is still untouched—is not one temple but the foundations of two, lying parallel to each other and facing the sea. The ground plans are typically Etruscan, and they date the older and smaller temple at about 500 B.C., the other perhaps twenty or thirty years later. Eight seasons of the most meticulous digging, photographing, testing, and restoring have produced a wealth of stuff of special interest because the site is a great rarity in Etruscology—it is not a cemetery. But nothing touches the discovery of July 8, 1964, in a niche between the two temples: the three tablets already mentioned, carefully folded and of pure gold, no more than one third to one half a millimeter in thickness, which, when opened, were revealed to have expertly engraved inscriptions in Punic and Etruscan on them. Even the bronze, gold-headed nails with which the tablets were affixed (conceivably to the doors of the older temple) were preserved. However, no dedicatory objects of any kind accompanied the tablets, and so one plausible suggestion has been offered that the older temple was taken down to be replaced by the larger one and the tablets deposited for permanent preservation on that occasion.

This idea must be treated with considerable reserve at present, as must most other inferences. That I am able to write anything at all detailed on the subject so soon after the discovery is a tribute to Professor Pallottino, who with his associates proceeded immediately to months of intensive study of the difficult documents. They have translated the Punic text without too many question marks:

> "To the lady Astarte. This is the sacred place made and given by Thefarie Velianas, king of Cisra, in the month of the Sacrifice of the Sun in gift within the temple and sanctuary [?] because Astarte has raised [him] with her hand [?], in the third year of his reign, in the month of Krr, on the day of the Burial of the Divinity. And the years of the statue of the goddess in her temple [are as many] as these stars."

The two Etruscan tablets between them seem to repeat most of the essential information of the Punic one and to elaborate a bit on the cult practices. The writing is in the local style of Caere, which was to be expected, and the dating previously suggested for the two temples on archaeological grounds, about 500–475 B.C., seems to fit the script well enough in a general way.

The overriding question, of course, is why did the ruler of an Etruscan city thirty miles from Rome bow down to Astarte (the Ishtar of the Bible), the chief goddess of the Carthaginians? Why, furthermore, does the longer of the Etruscan texts call her Astarte-Uni? That combination is of particular interest because Uni was identified with the Roman Juno and sometimes also assimilated to the Greek Hera, consort of Zeus. The three documents, no more than ninety words all together, thus plunge us into the very center of the political and cultural complex of western Mediterranean history at one of its most critical moments. But they give no further information, not even any clues, which must be sought elsewhere, in archaeological studies and among Greek and Roman writers.

Archaeology reveals connections between Italy and the eastern Mediterranean well back in the Bronze Age. In particular, southern Italy and Sicily received much pottery from Mycenaean Greece, and especially from the island of Rhodes, in the period 1400–1200 B.C. Then came a rather sudden and long "dark age," coinciding with a similar dark age in Greece, when the archaeological record is very impoverished and confused for about four hundred years. It was an age initiated by migrations from the north, presumably bringing in for the first time the peoples we call "Italic." That is to say, a fairly uniform material culture spread over most of Italy, and the inhabitants spoke closely related dialects belonging to the Italic branch of the Indo-European family of languages. Among them were the Sabines, Oscans, Umbrians, Samnites, Lucanians, and Latins. One of the latter, the Romans, ultimately conquered and absorbed all the rest.

At some point in the "dark age," but one which is impossible to fix, an alien element becomes visible, the Etruscans, whose language is not yet identifiable with any other but is surely not Indo-European. By about 700 B.C. much of the region now called Tuscany and Umbria, and some parts of Latium and Campania, were Etruscan in speech and culture. The Greeks and Romans in later centuries were firmly convinced that the Etruscans had come originally from western Asia Minor (modern Turkey); the Etruscans themselves seem to have believed that, too, and so do most (but not all) modern scholars.* Be that as it may, the "original Etruscans" were a relatively small group of men, and their civilization was a new creation fashioned in Italy. They apparently had a social system better fitted than the others for political expansion and organization, and they were able to exploit fully, and to their own advantage, the relatively rich metal deposits of the region.

Further advance to the south by the Etruscans was blocked by still a third element now in the picture, the Greeks. Beginning about 750 B.C., Greeks began to migrate westward and set up communities along the coast of southern Italy and Sicily, and later in Libya. At about the same time, or perhaps a little earlier, Phoenicians, the most intrepid and experienced sailors of them all, started to establish western trading posts and then genuine settlements in North Africa, on the western rim of Sicily, and on the Spanish coast. In time Carthage became the biggest, richest, and most powerful of these, and before 500 B.C. had brought all the western Phoenicians into its sphere.

In a rough way one can plot the groupings on a map (see page 108): the Italic peoples and the Etruscans in Italy, down to a line running east by south across the peninsula from the Bay of Naples, with the Etruscans also trying to edge their way by sea to Corsica and Sardinia; the Greeks in southern Italy, most of Sicily, and in Libya, also edging into southern France and for a time contending for Corsica and Sardinia; and the Carthaginians in the remaining spaces to the west and also joining in the struggle for the two larger islands. These were not proper national states—the Greeks not at all, and even the Etruscans, who were loosely federated, were never politically unified—and there were no national boundaries. The points of contact were fluid and shifting. (The later and never really justified image of a war to the death between Greeks and Romans on the one hand, and

*See "In Search of the Etruscans" by Raymond Bloch (HORIZON, May, 1960).

Besides the tablets, various terra cottas came to light at Pyrgi, all with Greek motifs. These fragments show Athena battling giants.

"barbarian" Etruscans and Carthaginians on the other, must not be read back into this earlier period, nor must the modern notions of racial superiority to which some historians are sadly prone.) It was from Cumae, on the Bay of Naples, for example, that the Greek alphabet, itself a borrowing from the Phoenician, was diffused to the Etruscans and the Latins. It was from the Etruscans that Rome received much of its first political and military organization and its first steps toward urbanization. Greek traders trafficked happily with Etruscans and Carthaginians, and there was a fair amount of settlement of Greeks in Carthaginian towns and vice versa.

This is the kind of relationship reflected in Strabo's brief statement about Pyrgi. No memory had survived that it was the Etruscans who had erected temples there, or of a cult of Astarte, hence the vague attribution to "Pelasgians." However, there can be no disputing the considerable Greek influence in Pyrgi both before and after the undoubtedly short-lived introduction of Astarte.

Trading often enough shaded off into piracy, and peace was disturbed often enough by short wars. But then, the same was true at the time among the Greek states themselves, in Greece proper and in the west, and among the Italic tribes, even within as closely related a group as the Latins. In the centuries when the Carthaginians and Etruscans were expanding and consolidating their positions almost on an imperial basis—roughly between 700 and 500 B.C.—they tried seriously to agree on spheres of influence, make treaties of friendship, define territories, and guarantee the rights of their traders. Because the Etruscans were not under a single rule, Carthage had to seek these goals by negotiating separately with individual Etruscan cities. The Italians do not seem to have been direct parties to such agreements because they were more backward and because they were accepted by the Carthaginians as fair prey for Etruscan expansion. And the Greeks were in a special position: they alone retained ties with

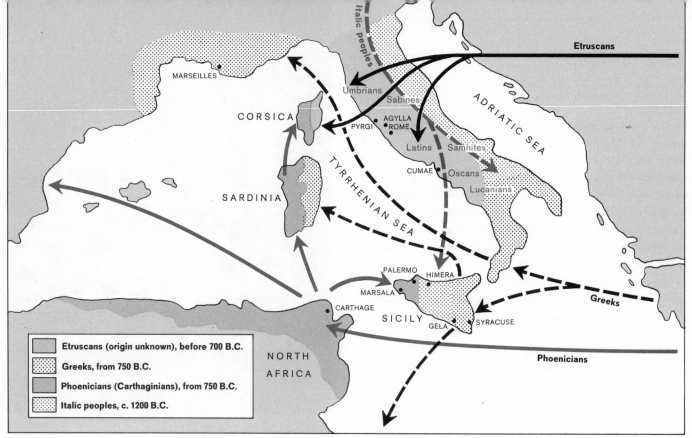

Italy and the western Mediterranean before the rise of Rome

their original homeland and continued to receive recruits for a long time, not always, as we shall see, of a type likely to contribute to peaceful relations with their neighbors.

With this as the background, we can set the Pyrgi documents within a framework of scattered but coherent events reported by various Greek and Roman writers (accepting, for the moment, the ancient statements as all strictly accurate):

540–530 B.C. Greeks from Phocaea in Asia Minor, who had penetrated farther west than any of their fellows (settling at Marseilles and spreading from there along the coast east to Nice and west into Spain), now entered on a phase of organized piracy against both Carthaginians and Etruscans, from a base on the island of Corsica. The victims joined forces to suppress the Phocaeans, and though the latter won a great naval battle in the waters off Sardinia, it was a Pyrrhic victory. The Phocaeans lost so many men and ships that they had to withdraw, leaving Corsica to the Etruscans and Sardinia to the Carthaginians. Herodotus tells a story that the Etruscans from Agylla (Caere) who were involved in the engagement, then stoned all their prisoners to death, bringing down the wrath of the gods on themselves. They finally sought advice from the Delphic oracle, who told them they could expiate their crime only by instituting regular sacrifices to the spirits of their victims and holding games in their honor. Which, Herodotus continues, they are still doing (that is, in the middle of the fifth century B.C.). And so we have further evidence, in the familiar guise of myth, of a Greek cult in the district of Caere, precisely in the period of the Pyrgi tablets.

524 B.C. The Etruscans, with the support of some of their Italic subjects, attacked Cumae, the oldest Greek settlement in the west and the most powerful Greek community in Campania. They failed, and this marked the end of any serious Etruscan effort to expand southward. It also set off bitter class conflict within Cumae.

509–508 B.C. Rome revolted from Etruscan overlordship, ex-

pelled her Etruscan king, Tarquinius Superbus, and set itself up as an independent republic under the Senate and two consuls. (It is characteristic of the tradition that the revolt should be sparked by a personal affront, the rape of the matron Lucretia by the king's youngest son, Sextus, an incident that has become famous in drama and song.) One of the first acts of the new Roman regime was to sign a treaty with Carthage, the effect of which was to define and delimit the movement of Roman traders in Libya, Sardinia, and Carthaginian Sicily, and to obtain recognition by Carthage of Rome's political claims in Latium.

494 B.C. After the Persians had suppressed the revolt of the Ionian Greeks in Asia Minor, many Phocaeans fled west under a buccaneering leader named Dionysius and established a base in Sicily from which they resumed the traditional western Phocaean game of piracy against Carthaginian and Etruscan shipping.

480 B.C. The Carthaginians suffered a major military defeat at the hands of Greek forces in Sicily, at the battle of Himera on the northern coast of the island. The background was as follows: the Carthaginians had never made any attempt to settle in, or to control, Sicily, being satisfied with stations located at modern Marsala and Palermo on the sea route from North Africa to Europe. However, in a power struggle among the Sicilian Greeks, the Carthaginians were invited in—and that must be underscored —by the weaker forces as a counterweight, only to be crushed.

In this context the Pyrgi documents become intelligible. The last quarter of the sixth century B.C. marked the turning point in Etruscan history. The defeat at Cumae and the revolt of Rome heralded the slow breakup of Etruscan rule that was to follow, though another three hundred years were to elapse before there were no more independent Etruscan cities left at all. Carthage, which had established a reasonable modus vivendi with the Etruscans, could not completely ignore these new developments and allowed itself to be involved, however slightly. Hence the treaty with Rome and the temple of Astarte at Pyrgi. What we cannot know on present evidence is the immediate history behind the activities of the donor, Thefarie Velianas, whose name is inscribed on the tablets (incidentally, Thefarie is the Latin "Tiberius," one more instance of cultural assimilation). Was he a legitimate ruler—king or chief magistrate—of Caere, or a tyrant who had seized power? Was he the first to bring Astarte to Pyrgi, and did he dedicate his golden tablets in the hope of winning Carthaginian support? Or was that the price he was paying for help already given? Help against whom? Whatever the answers, Caere and Pyrgi prospered. They were still rich and under Etruscan rule when Dionysius of Syracuse looted them in 394 B.C. It is anyone's guess as to which deity was in possession of the temple then—mine is that Astarte had long since departed and that the cult was Greco-Etruscan, though perhaps that of Uni-Hera rather than that of Eileithyia.

From the longer historical view, of course, the most important event of the whole complex is the emergence of an independent Rome. The Roman traditions about their own origins and early history did not attain their final form for another five hundred years. No one doubts that the account is filled with improbabilities and outright fictions: it is enough to point out that the city had two different—and equally legendary—founders, Romulus and Aeneas. But how much truth remains at the kernel?

In bald outline the Roman tradition is that the city was founded in 753 B.C., came under Etruscan rule in 616 (the king being Tarquinius Priscus), freed itself in 509, proceeded to consolidate its position as head of the Latins, and then never looked back. There were few ancient cities without legendary founders, and in this case we need not take either the stories or the date seriously. Archaeology does suggest, however, that the Capitoline and Palatine hills were the first centers of occupation, and this is where the tradition also locates Rome's "foundation." From the hills, settlement spread to the old Forum, which they cradled, and to the "sacred way," running east from the Forum. So far there is no serious argument among modern historians. Trouble begins when the Forum was leveled, given a pebble floor and then a proper pavement, and when "developed architecture" (as distinct from huts) made its appearance. According to the distinguished Swedish archaeologist Einar Gjerstad, these fundamental new developments fall within the period 575–450 B.C., and he reconstructs the history this way: Rome was not really "founded" as an urban community until 575, when the earlier separate villages on the hills were united; then came Etruscan rule under kings, and ultimately their expulsion in 450.

Fifty years one way or another does not make much difference, especially when one remembers that archaeological dating must always allow for at least that much margin of error. But this scheme creates more problems than it solves. I shall mention only two of the difficulties. For one thing, it contradicts the one piece of documentation which the later creators of the Roman tradition had to work from—a list, going back to the beginning of the Republic, of the two consuls for each year. Whatever may have been the truth about anything earlier or about occurrences later,

that bare list existed, and its seems arbitrary to dismiss all the names of the first half-century as a later invention when there is no good reason why anyone should have wanted to take such liberties merely to shift the establishment of the republic from 450 to 509.

Second, the proposed new chronology does not fit well into the historical framework of the whole region as I have sketched it. And that is where the Pyrgi tablets help, by shedding new light on Carthage's direct connection with internal developments in Italy. There have always been historians who disbelieved the treaty of 509 or 508 between Rome and Carthage, as does the Gjerstad school, on the grounds that Rome was too insignificant to be allied with so great a power and that it had no trade of its own worthy of the name, thus making nonsense of the trading provisions of the treaty. These would be cogent arguments in isolation. They lose their force when one remembers that Carthage had been writing just such treaties with many Etruscan cities. There is, then, nothing implausible about a renewal of the provisions, repeated more or less automatically, after Rome broke from Etruscan overlordship. That fits the position about 500 B.C., but not the international situation half a century later. It fits the date of the Pyrgi temples and tablets. If a ruler of Caere could be recognized by Carthage at that time, so could a new regime in Rome.

It is necessary to underscore the point that there can be no defense of the details of the Roman tradition, not even of what was said to have actually happened in 509. There was no "expulsion of the Etruscans" then. There was a political change which was to have an impact on the future that no contemporary could conceivably have imagined, but it was not a change that would leave any traces in the archaeological record, and especially not in the middle of Rome, a city with an absolutely continuous history of crowded habitation ever since. Failure to appreciate that seems to me to be the big fallacy in the Gjerstad argument.

The border line between a "legitimate" king and what the Greeks called a "tyrant" was a very thin one. Struggles between tyrants and aristocracies were going on all over the Greek world in the sixth century, and also in Italy, Sicily, and apparently in Carthage. Often the lower classes sided with the tyrant, as in Cumae after their victory over the Etruscans. That may have been the situation in Pyrgi, too, and in Rome. The Roman nobles who threw out the tyrant-king Tarquinius Superbus were of mixed Latin-Etruscan (and probably also Sabine) stock. That is why men with unmistakably Etruscan names still appear in the consular lists for the next half-century, until Etruscan names as such were either fully Latinized in Rome, or dropped. The Roman plebs, there is some reason to think, would have preferred rule by Etruscans to rule by their own nobles. Eventually, and for obvious reasons, these aspects of the establishment of the republic fell from the tradition, to be replaced by a clean-cut patriotic story of noble Romans and brutal, licentious Etruscans.

M. I. Finley's articles on ancient people and places appear often in HORIZON. *He is an American classicist who lectures at Cambridge.*

MOTHER
to the
FATHERLAND

The Empress and her old enemy, Frederick II, play "diplomatic chess" as Mars looks on

CONTINUED FROM PAGE 23

the Empress made Cytherean pleasures extremely difficult . . ."

Actually, this was only because Casanova did not know the ropes. The great lords and cavaliers of the city who had formerly set up a pretty mistress in a little house in the country—a custom that had become far too dangerous—would now arrange for her to be hired as an extra chambermaid by some elderly respectable marquise of their acquaintance who had not forgotten her own youth; when the lord's coach stood half the night outside a mansion door, nobody thought a thing about it, least of all the chastity police. An occasional "chambermaid" was caught, of course, had her hair shaved off, and was stood in the pillory. On the whole, however, there was a great rush into the chambermaid market.

Certainly the Chastity Commission did not deter in the least the Empress's own husband. During the Carnival season of 1756 Franz took as his mistress a gray-eyed beauty of the court, Princess Wilhelmina Auersperg. The attachment lasted until his death ten years later.

The Princess was no ordinary rival. Daughter of a field marshal of the Empire, she belonged to one of the noblest families at court and had married into another; she was, besides, supremely lovely. Franz gave her a country house near the palace at Laxenburg, south of Vienna, and began to devote more and more time to the chase. The Princess presided at lively little supper parties at Laxenburg, with covers laid for ten or twelve and all ceremony banished. Like Franz, she adored the gaming table, and her lover undertook to pay her enormous gambling debts.

In July of 1765 the imperial couple set out from the Hofburg by coach to attend the wedding in Innsbruck of their third son, Leopold, to a princess of Spain. The Empress was unaccountably nervous; they were late starting out and Franz made her very cross by turning the carriage back to give one more farewell kiss to his favorite little daughter, Maria Antonia, who was then ten years old. Several weeks later, in Innsbruck, on his way to a gala performance of an opera, Franz suddenly staggered, put his hand to his head, collapsed, and died within minutes.

Although Maria Theresa was only forty-eight years old, in a blooming and vigorous prime, she never took off her mourning. The pale gold ringlets that had entranced the Hungarian nobles at Pressburg, threaded now with gray, were snipped off and combed back flat under a black crepe cap. She moved out of those joyous rococo rooms in the Hofburg into a black-draped apartment on the third floor, with a trap door that opened so she could hear Mass from the chapel beneath. She never wore her jewels again, never masked again, nor danced, nor took a lover. She forbade the ladies of the court to rouge for the whole period of mourning.

A few days after Franz's death the court exchequer brought the Empress a note for 200,000 florins—a gambling debt of the Princess Auersperg found among Franz's papers. The Empress ordered it paid. The Princess, meantime, was particularly bitter about the ban on rouge: "Is it possible that one cannot be mistress of one's own face?"

At Schönbrunn and elsewhere, Maria Theresa's baker's dozen of blond, blue-eyed boys and girls gaze brightly and hopefully out of their portraits, as if the future could hold nothing for a Habsburg child but the sunniest of summer weather. Against the identical Schönbrunn terrace background the eight pretty girls smile out of the pictures, in splendid gowns all lace, brocade, and satin bows, with the five handsome boys in periwigs and velvet breeches—quite the image of the Ideal Ruling Family, even to the two puppies frisking in the foreground.

No wonder they were the talk of Europe. No other eighteenth-century court had anything quite like them. In Potsdam the hated Frederick kept a strictly male ménage and communicated with his wife only by letter. In St. Petersburg the childless spinster Czarina Elizabeth hired lovers to keep her company. At Versailles there was Pompadour to amuse the aging Louis XV, along with a batch of unattractive and unmarried princesses.

For years the nursery wing that occupied part of the ground floor of Schönbrunn bustled with activity, with the drone of children reciting lessons, the tinkle of harpsichord and soprano scales, the clink of little boys practicing fencing. But Maria Theresa had little time to spare for her children. They might kiss her hand at certain hours of the day; occasionally she would hurry down to the schoolroom to see how one or another of the children was absorbing his lesson. Mostly she communicated her wishes on their upbringing in writing—precise instructions to each tutor and governess, even to the prayers the children were to recite each morning and evening.

The nurses and governesses and *ayos* (head preceptors) were usually widowed countesses or retired court officials, chosen less for their understanding and experience with children than for their irreproachable piety and knowledge of court protocol. Besides the chief tutors and governesses—one for each child or two—a regiment of special teachers came and went to give instructions in dancing, music, languages, writing.

Discipline was strict; there was no permissiveness in the imperial nursery. Nor did a child have any privacy; a tutor or governess or chamberlain was watching every hour of the day. The children's daily schedules were crammed as full as their mother's. Delicate, nervous Josepha, who broke too easily into tears, studied in the course of each day German, Latin, Spanish, Italian, history, grammar, religion, and writing. At four o'clock her dancing master came, after which she recited her Rosary "very loudly," then ate a simple supper—"soup and one other dish," her mother's precise instructions read. She saw her family only on Sundays, when she could join them for church and dinner. Josepha's governess had got a firmly worded message from the imperial mother that the girl's bad habits "must be uprooted immediately and thoroughly. . . . I cannot flatter myself that I can be successful with her until the source of her trouble, her violent temper and her selfishness, have been restrained. When she is even spoken to, she becomes so irritated that she is ready to weep in anger."

The eldest boy, Joseph, showed great promise. He was not a quick learner like his attractive, mercurial brother Charles, but he had the kind of dogged mind that never loses what it has once grasped. *Der Starrkopf*, "the stubborn one," his mother called him. Once Maria Theresa ordered that Joseph be punished by a caning. When his chamberlains protested that no archduke ever got spanked, she retorted, "That's plain to see from their manners," but she rescinded the order.

Periodically she wrote long, detailed letters to her daughters, reviewing their manners and conduct. To fourteen-year-old Caroline, who had requested a change of governesses, she wrote permitting the change but reprimanding her severely for saying her prayers carelessly and for being rude to her ladies in waiting while they were dressing her. Her instructions for queenhood were explicit: "You are conscientiously to continue your exercises in music, painting, history, geography, and Latin. You must never be lazy, for indolence is dangerous for everyone and especially for you. You must occupy your mind . . ."

As they grew older the children began to appear in court society. Throngs came to watch them dine in public with their parents in the gilded Hall of Mirrors under a gold-embroidered canopy. On birthdays and name days and other special occasions they appeared in private theatricals and ballets in the palace theatre; the foreign envoys exchanged malicious smiles when poor shy Joseph fumbled and swallowed his words as he recited a poem one of the ladies of the court had composed in honor of his mother's birthday.

They are scarcely out of the nursery before their mother is juggling marriage plans. These thirteen children —three of the sixteen Maria Theresa bore had died in infancy—represented an incalculable political capital. For twenty years their marriages absorbed a great share of the Empress's time and planning. Into these marriages she wove the great political theme of her reign—alliance with Austria's ancient enemy, France, against the new enemy, Prussia; through them she made a subtle reconquest of the Italian states lost by her father's inept statesmanship.

The matter of heirs having top priority, Crown Prince Joseph was married first—to Princess Isabella of Parma, a granddaughter of the king of France.

Joseph was shy with women; he had little ease of manner or small talk. But he had the rarest good fortune for a crown prince—he fell deeply in love with the wife his parents had chosen for him. Isabella had been perfectly trained for the job of royal wife. She took infinite pains to charm her awkward young husband, to draw him out, to give him pleasure in her company. The whole family was enchanted with her; Joseph succumbed completely. For a serious boy, deep in the French philosophers, Isabella seemed an ideal mate. Instead of the typical *romans larmoyants* of the century, Isabella was reading Bossuet and John Law; her own writings show a remarkably profound understanding of the political situation of her day.

But if she was the nearly perfect wife, still it was not Joseph who commanded Isabella's deepest affection but his sister, Marie Christine, whom the family called Mimi. Exactly the same age, eighteen, the two princesses, the dark Italian and the blond Austrian, walked together in the Schönbrunn gardens, exchanged endless confidences, sang and made music together, painted portraits of one another, and even though they met each day, exchanged long, loving, intimate letters.

To Mimi, Isabella would write: "I am writing to you again, cruel sister, though I have only just left you. I cannot bear waiting to know my fate, and to learn whether you consider me a person worthy of your love, or whether you would like to fling me into the river. . . . I can think of nothing but that I am madly in love."

And a little later: "I am told that the day begins with God. I, however, begin the day by thinking of the object of my love, for I think of her incessantly."

Together with that violent friendship, a deep melancholy laid hold of Joseph's pretty young wife; her letters reveal an increasing preoccupation with death. There is no evidence that Joseph noticed anything unusual, but to friends and to her lady in waiting, Isabella declared that she would die soon, and added that the little daughter, Theresa, whom she had borne to Joseph, would not long remain behind.

Certainly she did not have to seek death out: it was never long absent from any eighteenth-century household. When she had been married just three years and was pregnant with her second child, Isabella was stricken with smallpox. Joseph, who had been immunized by a childhood attack, watched by her bedside in anguish as she grew worse each day. She died in November, 1763, at twenty-one.

The official court mourning period was not yet over before Joseph's mother was broaching new marriage plans: it was absolutely essential for an anointed successor to produce heirs. Absorbed in his grief, the young wid-

"The Queen of Hungary Stript," an English cartoon of 1741, bawdily shows Maria Theresa at the mercy of other powers.

ower at first refused to consider them, but finally gave in —looking over with indifference the distasteful choices offered from among the few available Catholic princesses.

His second marriage to the Bavarian princess Josepha took place at Schönbrunn in 1765. It was anything but gay, though the Empress tried her level best to make it so. Even the Viennese could not summon up a festive spirit. The bride was two years older than her husband; cynics hinted that the Bavarian Elector had swindled the Habsburgs and sent his aunt instead of his sister. Besides being awkward and not at all clever, Josepha was downright plain; her whole face and body were covered with scorbutic sores. The family ignored her, except for the Emperor Franz, who was kind to everyone.

As for Joseph, he simply couldn't bear her. He had the balcony connecting their two apartments partitioned off, and spent as much time as possible traveling. He wrote his mother: "Excuse me for not writing to my wife.

There is nothing to say to her; wind and rain cannot fill up a page." And later: "They want me to have children. How can one have them? If I could put the tip of my finger on the tiniest part of her body which is not covered with pimples, I would try to have children."

Melancholy and chronically ailing, the unfortunate Josepha spent her days trying cures at the nearby spa of Baden. In the terrible smallpox epidemic of 1767 Josepha got the disease in its most malignant form and died within days. In pity for the girl, the Empress visited her bedside during her illness. It was then that Maria Theresa contracted smallpox herself, and lay so close to death that the last rites were given her. She recovered, however: it would take more than smallpox to kill her.

That decade of the 1760's was a terrible one for the Empress. Her favorite son, Charles, a charming boy of sixteen, died of smallpox, and so did gentle twelve-year-old Joanna. Both Joseph's wives had died of the pox, and it was in the middle of this decade that Maria Theresa herself became a widow.

Yet amid her sorrows she continued with her marriage plans. The oldest daughter, Marianna, crippled apparently from birth, was destined by her mother for a convent. Vivacious, attractive Marie Christine, called Mimi, the second daughter, was her mother's favorite. Her parents had wanted to betroth Mimi to the French Duc de Chablais, but Mimi held out firmly for her own choice of suitor—Duke Albert of Saxony, a younger son with neither fortune nor prospect of a throne. She got her way; it was a deeply happy match.

The third daughter, Elizabeth, was the great beauty of the family and a born coquette. ("So long as she pleases someone, whether it is a soldier on guard duty or a prince, she is content," her mother once wrote Joseph.) Everyone was certain that a brilliant match, probably with a ruling monarch, was in store for Elizabeth. The Empress turned down a proposal from Stanislas, ex-king of Poland, certain that something better would turn up. When King Louis XV of France lost his wife, it seemed possible that the new Franco-Austrian alliance that was arranged by Kaunitz might be cemented by a match between the blooming, young Elizabeth and the elderly monarch.

But in the autumn of 1767 Elizabeth, too, came down with smallpox. It was said that as the girl grew more ill, she asked for a looking glass so that she could look one last time at her pretty face. She did not die, but when she held a mirror again, it was to a face horribly ravaged, every trace of her beauty destroyed. Her suitors melted away. The lecherous old king of France slyly sent a court painter to do her portrait; the marriage overtures were dropped. Frantically Elizabeth called in doctors and quacks, tried medicines and salves. When it became clear at last that she was doomed to spinsterhood, Maria Theresa bestowed on her daughter the only life possible for damaged princesses and youngest sons—the Church. As titular head of an order for aged ladies in Innsbruck, Elizabeth continued to live in the Hofburg, a bitter spinster, angry with the world and with her fate.

There were, meantime, the younger children to plan for. Little Joanna, who died at twelve, had already been betrothed to Ferdinando, child king of Naples and younger son of the Bourbon king of Spain. Maria Theresa, determined not to let the central Italian kingdom slip from her, hastened to betroth another daughter, the gentle Josepha, to take her sister's place. Most disquieting rumors had reached the Vienna court about the boy monarch of Naples. Ferdinando's older brother was an imbecile, and Ferdinando himself of so unpromising a mentality that his father had decided not to submit him to the rigors of an education. He could barely read, spoke only the Neapolitan dialect, and cared for nothing but hunting and outdoor games.

But if Josepha sulked over her prospective marriage, her mother saw her own duty clearly. To Josepha's governess she wrote firmly: "I consider Josepha a sacrifice to politics, and, if she fulfills her duty to her husband and her God, I shall be content."

In October of 1767 the preparations for Josepha's departure had been made, her trousseau, including a hundred dresses from Paris, was in readiness, and Vienna was thronged with wedding guests. Josepha had been born on her brother Joseph's name day, and she was his favorite little sister. He had promised to accompany her on her bridal journey as far as the city of Florence. A few days before the wedding, the Empress took Josepha with her into the Kapuziner crypt to pay a farewell visit to the tombs of the Habsburg dead. Josepha had begged not to go; her attendants declared that she wept in the carriage that drove her to the church and shivered while she knelt praying in the chilly crypt. Within a few hours Josepha, too, lay mortally sick of smallpox; she died on the day she would have departed to be Queen of Naples. The whole court whispered that she had caught the disease in the crypt where the body of her sister-in-law, the unlucky Bavarian Josepha, had festered unembalmed since the previous May.

Maria Theresa did not abandon her plans for the throne of Naples. As soon as decency permitted, she betrothed her next-to-youngest daughter, fifteen-year-old Caroline, to Ferdinando. She was neither so pretty nor so docile as her sisters had been, but she was plump, pink-cheeked, and possessed a good deal of her mother's robust spirit.

Caroline plainly did not want to marry Ferdinando. Probably word had reached Vienna of the boy king's behavior the previous autumn when he got news in Naples of his second fiancée's death. Bored and sulky because he was not permitted to go hunting that day, he made life miserable for his attendants until a way was devised to amuse him. When the English ambassador arrived at the palace in Naples to pay a sympathy call, he found Ferdinando and his suite playing funeral with a young gentleman of the court in the role of the archduchess in funeral robes, his face daubed with chocolate to resemble smallpox, and a great deal of accompanying hilarity.

In spite of her protests, Caroline was married by proxy in Vienna. It was reported that she wept bitterly as the bridal procession made its stately way over the Alps and finally across the border into the then large kingdom of Naples. Her elder brother Leopold, Grand Duke of Tuscany, met her in Bologna and saw to it that she was delivered into the hands of Ferdinando's people for a formal ceremony. Although Leopold wrote his mother soothingly that Caroline was "a most amiable little Queen," he added that she had been seized by a violent fit of trembling during the ceremony, and that "not for a whole kingdom would I want to live through such a scene again."

Caroline, after only a few months of marriage, wrote that life was a martyrdom: "I now know what marriage is, and I have a deep pity for Antoinette, who has yet to experience marriage. I admit frankly that I would rather die than be forced to experience again what I have gone through. . . ." And yet, in spite of everything, Caroline took her mother's words to heart, made the best of her lot, managed to improve her husband's manners a little, learned how to get what she wanted, and finally herself became the mother and grandmother of kings, queens, and empresses. When her brother Joseph visited her in Naples two or three years later, things were already better, and he assured his mother the pair were getting along nicely.

Ferdinando's amusements continued to be decidedly unregal: "Five or six court ladies, my sister, the King and I," Joseph wrote, "began to play blindman's bluff and other games . . . Throughout these the King distributes blows and smacks the ladies' behinds without distinction." On their way to the opera, the king seized one of Caroline's gloves, pretended to hide it, and actually threw it out of the window. "My sister behaved with great moderation," Joseph continued, "considering that a few days previously Ferdinando had also thrown her best muff into the fire."

"Er ist ein recht guter Narr," Caroline remarked philosophically ("He's a pretty good fool"). As for the king, he told Joseph over and over again that he could not be more contented with his wife.

There were just two marriageable sisters left in the Hofburg: Amalia, and the youngest sister, Antoinette. Pretty twenty-two-year-old Amalia had been a decoration in court society for several years. She had a pleasant coloratura voice, danced with grace, and already had her eye on a husband: the Bavarian duke Charles of Zweibrücken, an eminently suitable match. By this time Joseph was sharing the throne with his mother; he had designs on Bavaria, and he felt the marriage would be politically awkward. Perhaps he had personal reasons for wishing to see his sister marry his beloved first wife's brother, the Duke of Parma; it would mean, in any case, one more Habsburg sharing an Italian throne. Amalia had neither the will power nor the persuasive gifts of her sister Mimi; in the end she submitted to the marriage arranged for her. Unhappily, the bridegroom turned out to be an immature boy of seventeen, a clear case of arrested development, and the marriage was far more disastrous than Caroline's. Within a year Amalia's conduct was the gossip of every court in Europe.

Soon after Amalia's marriage, the Empress became totally absorbed in the grand climax of all her matrimonial plans: that of uniting her youngest daughter, Maria Antonia, called Antoinette, with the Dauphin of France.

By the time the little Antoinette was born into an enormous family that already had grown-up children, discipline in the nursery had considerably relaxed, and, as often happens in such families, everyone took turns spoiling the child. Antoinette and her sister Caroline, nearly of an age, shared the same lessons and the same governess. Together the girls ran about the gardens of Schönbrunn, skipped their lessons when they could, and enjoyed themselves thoroughly. Antoinette was eleven when her betrothal to the Dauphin was officially announced. People began to bow and scrape and address her as "Madame Antoine," and her mother began to wonder how she could squeeze into that pretty little head all the knowledge, common sense, and good judgment she would need to make her way skillfully through the temptations and intrigues of the court of France. Antoinette got a whole new set of teachers to improve her French diction and her knowledge of French history. But it was her earlier masters who left the deepest impression: her music teacher, the great Gluck, and her almost equally celebrated ballet master, the Frenchman Noverre. Under his direction she had danced in ballets in the Court Theatre; that wonderful grace of movement which enabled her to outshine far more beautiful women at the French court was certainly part of his training.

The wedding was probably the most brilliant of a brilliant century. French and Austrian officials had labored over knotty questions of mutual protocol for a solid year and had finally given up in despair. In the end, the French ambassador, the Marquis of Durfort, stayed away from the wedding supper because the bride's brother-in-law, Duke Albert, was given precedence over him at table. On the whole, however, everything went smoothly.

There were the preliminary ceremonies—the solemn audience in the Hofburg on April 16, with the court in full dress, when the French ambassador asked the hand of Madame Antoine as consort for Monseigneur the Dauphin; the gala performance at the Court Theatre of a new comedy by Marivaux and a new ballet by Noverre; the Act of Renunciation in the Hofburg, when the Archduchess signed away all her rights to the Habsburg inheritance; the grand nuptial ball at Belvedere Palace, when six thousand guests in mask danced away the night. And finally the wedding itself, in the Augustinerkirche, where the bride's parents and most of her sisters had been married, with the bride's brother Ferdinand standing proxy for the groom.

Two days later, bathed in tears, Marie Antoinette bade good-bye to her mother and set off in a splendid procession of carriages for Versailles, certainly with a lighter heart than either Caroline or Amalia had done, and with her mother's last instructions, several closely written pages of that famous *Règlement*, to guide her first steps in France. Of her bridegroom she knew far less than Caroline had known of Ferdinando, and certainly had not heard the judgment passed on the future Louis XVI by the Austrian ambassador to France, Count Mercy d'Argenteau: "Nature seems to have denied everything to M. le Dauphin." The marriage and the production of little Habsburg-Bourbons was to be the very keystone in the great Austrian-French alliance, the happy conclusion of the centuries-long feud between the houses of Austria and France. Well prepared by her mother as to the exact meaning of marriage, the pretty little bride could scarcely guess that she would remain a wife in name only for some seven years.

Back in Vienna the golden palace of Schönbrunn had almost emptied. The last marriage of all was that of Archduke Ferdinand to Beatrix, heiress of Modena: another valuable Italian throne brought into the family. The youngest boy, Maximilian, who had no inclination for marriage, took holy orders and became Archbishop of Cologne, one of the richest and fattest prelates in Europe, and—handily for future Habsburgs—a member of the Electoral College.

There was a last bitter grief for the aging Empress. Her first little granddaughter, Theresa, child of Joseph and Isabella, died just before Antoinette's wedding. It was said, cruelly, that the child had contracted her fatal pneumonia running about in her grandmother's chilly rooms. She had been a particularly merry and attractive child. Joseph, doomed now to lonely and childless widowhood, wrote the little girl's governess: "To be no longer father seems more than I can bear. . . . I shall miss my daughter all the remaining days of my life. . . . One thing I beg of you, let me have the little white woollen dress with the embroidery of flowers that she has been wearing indoors, and likewise some of her attempts at writing, which I will keep with her mother's writings . . ." It must have been a lonely household, suddenly without young voices at all and not a great deal to laugh about.

The Archduchesses Marianna and Elizabeth, two aging spinsters, quarreled constantly and ate at separate tables, each waited on by her own servants. Elizabeth, with her ravaged, pock-marked face, would often be so angry at the world that she refused to speak to anyone for days at a time. When she had an ulcer in her cheek and the British ambassador paid her a visit of sympathy, she laughed at him and said, "Believe me, for an archduchess of forty years who isn't married, a hole in the cheek is an amusement. No event which breaks the *ennui* of my life is a misfortune."

Since his father's death, Joseph had shared the throne as co-regent with his mother. It was a stormy partnership. Both stubborn, strong personalities, mother and son were separated by one of the most intellectually volcanic generations in human history. Maria Theresa, child of Baroque times, devout Catholic, represented the best of a dying order—the old conservative, paternalistic monarchy. Joseph, who had cut his teeth on the French philosophers, longed to enlighten and revolutionize a whole feudal empire overnight. "With the best will, we do not understand one another," his mother wrote him. They clashed constantly when they were together in the Hofburg. To escape those constant quarrels, Joseph traveled as much and as far as he could, to France and Italy, to Bohemia and Hungary, Poland and Russia.

He lectured his brother-in-law, Ferdinando of Naples, on the French philosophers; he persuaded his other brother-in-law, the French king, to undergo the little operation that would finally enable him to perform his duty as a husband. He annoyed his mother by visiting dangerous French radicals—Jean Jacques Rousseau in a Paris garret, the naturalist Buffon. And he dined with her bitterest enemy, Frederick the Great.

Maria Theresa, meantime, was growing stout and dropsical. She wore gaiters around her legs and used a glass to peer at persons a few paces away. She had quite lost her looks. The smallpox she caught at her daughter-in-law's bedside had left her deeply scarred. On a journey to Pressburg, driving at her usual breakneck speed, the carriage overturned and the Empress was flung out on her face in the loose gravel, an accident that cost her the last vestige of her beauty, and, very nearly, her eyesight. Her profile on the silver ducats of the last years of her reign looks like that of an old, tough Roman senator.

She kept her high color, was indeed always so warm that she rarely put down her fan and kept her windows open night and day. Joseph had to put on a fur coat to visit his mother's chambers. She never lost her humor. When she stood chatting one day with her chamberlain,

Count Sinzendorff, who was as old as she but thin as a rail and very rheumatic, she dropped a petition she was showing him and she motioned to him to pick it up. "*Hélas, Madame*" he replied sadly, "*il y a vingt années que je ne suis courbé*" ("I haven't bent over in twenty years"). Bursting into laughter at the plight of two old souls, one so fat and one so thin that neither could stoop, the Empress rang for a groom to retrieve the paper.

She still loved Schönbrunn, and as soon as spring came moved into the garden rooms on the first floor, painted with exotic landscapes in the eighteenth-century fashion. She had only to open her door and walk out by a graveled path to the Gloriette, the pavilion that crowns the hill behind the gardens, her dispatch box strapped to her waist.

On the eighteenth of every month, the anniversary of her husband's death, she went down into the Kapuziner crypt to visit her dead, that growing company that quite fills the majestic tomb room she had built. On November

"*Maria Theresa's last day*": the Empress died in her chair
PHOTO ALPENLAND—ALBERTINA, VIENNA

3, 1780, she wrote her last letter to Marie Antoinette: "At my age I need help and consolation and I am losing everything I love, one after the other. I am crushed by it all."

She stayed at Schönbrunn as late as she could in the autumn of 1780, and then she too caught a chill in the cold, vast rooms. When she moved back to the Hofburg in early November, she was ill already and breathing with difficulty. She never went to bed, but sat propped up on a chaise, in an old dressing gown of her late husband's, giving last instructions to Joseph as if he were a little boy.

Several years spent in Vienna as the wife of an American State Department officer whetted Dorothy McGuigan's interest in Maria Theresa and the innumerable Habsburgs who ruled before and after her. The result is her first book, The Habsburgs, *from which this excerpt is taken. It will be published this summer by Doubleday & Company.*

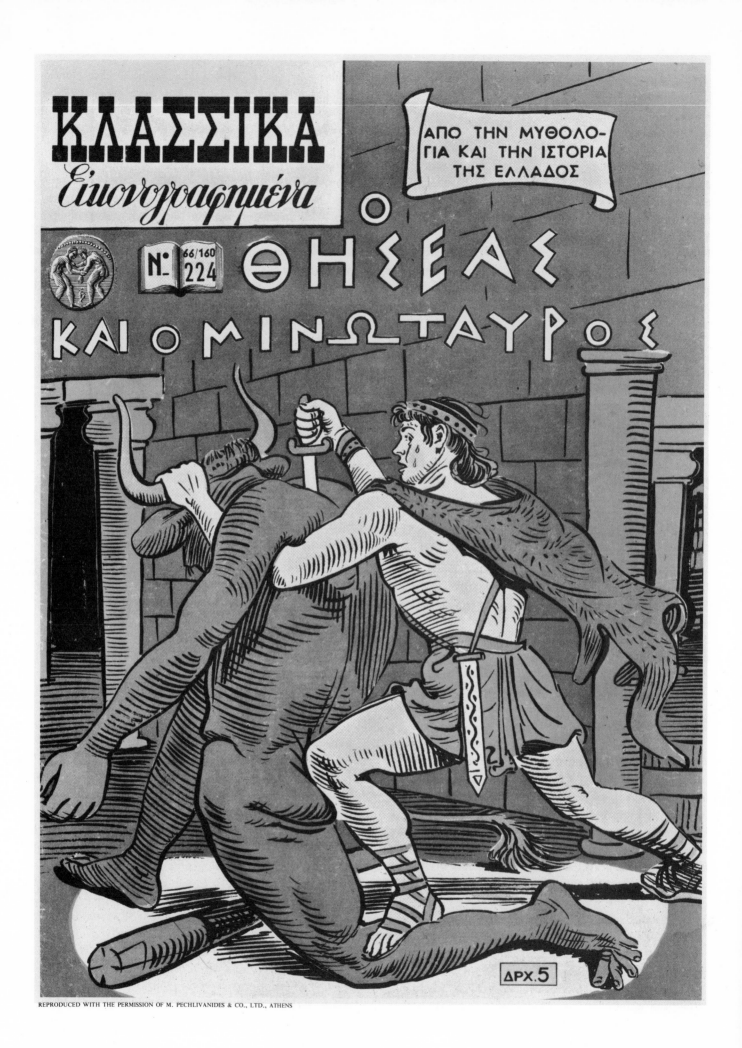

116

Classical Comics

Long before the infant Superman arrived on earth from his home on the planet Krypton, or young Billy Batson learned the magic word SHAZAM, which turned him into Captain Marvel, making him invulnerable to the attacks of master criminals, a race of glorious heroes flourished in ancient Greece. The men among them were as strong and handsome as Superman, and the women as beautiful as Wonder Woman herself. These "godlike heroes," as the ancient poet Hesiod called them, have passed from the scene, leaving behind "evil strife . . . and the grim battle's roar"; but they have not been forgotten, for great poets from Homer onward, and great artists from Phidias to Picasso, have recorded their deeds. And today Athenian artists—who could be descendants of those men who brought the art of Greek vase painting to such great heights—are busily at work recalling the ancient glories of their race. At the office where the Greek editions of that old American favorite, *Classic Comics*, are published, these dedicated antiquarians put in long hours drawing straining biceps and heroic fists and lettering balloons with the Greek equivalents of "Let's go!" "Pow!" and "Argghh!"

Into the Labyrinth

"Theseus and the Minotaur" is one of these classic productions, whose authors have taken a few liberties with the ancient myth. Their dread Minotaur emits a cowlike "Moo," and their hero, in true comic-book style, has acquired a boy assistant—in this case a rather loutish lad named Macha. At right is a climactic episode from the story, with Theseus in the labyrinth, tracking down the Minotaur.

THE DIALOGUE

1) MACHA: I'm exhausted. I've lost my hands! Where's my legs?
   THESEUS: Let's stay here in the dark so the beast will come out. Macha, you go ahead so he'll come toward you.
   MINOTAUR: Moo!
2) MACHA: Oh, what shall I do?
3) THESEUS: Go ahead, don't be scared!
   MACHA: Right now?
4) MACHA: Hey there, little Minotaur. . . .

The happy outcome of the adventure, Theseus's killing of the Minotaur, is shown opposite—on the comic book's cover.

Heracles and the Serpents

An enemy once changed Billy Batson into an infant, rendering him powerless, for he could no longer say "SHAZAM!" and become Captain Marvel; all he could say was "tha-tam." Greek heroes, even as infants, were made of sterner stuff. Heracles, the greatest of them all, enjoyed his first triumph while he was still in his cradle. The adventure is shown at the left.

THE DIALOGUE

1) NURSEMAID: Oh, I've forgotten my weaving. Let me go get it; it will just take a moment.

2) (*Meanwhile, the goddess Hera, jealous as usual because she knew her husband Zeus was in love with Heracles's mother Alcmene, sent two poisonous snakes to kill Heracles.*

3) *This is no ordinary baby, however, but the child of Zeus, and he strangles the snakes.*)

4) NURSEMAID AND GUARDS: Help! Help!

5) ALCMENE: Tell me, just how did all this happen?

6) THE PROPHET TIRESIAS: Well, Queen, I got here first because I heard the servants shouting, and I found both snakes on the ground, choked to death. Heracles strangled them with his hands. Oh, Father Zeus, glory to you who sent a hero to the world! Heracles is Zeus's son and when he grows up he will be glorified. He will live on because Zeus is his guardian . . .

Tiresias's prophecy came true, and Heracles grew up to become a champion of the oppressed. Two more of his astounding adventures are seen on the opposite page. At the top, he brings his friend's wife Alcestis back from the dead. In order to do this, he has to wrestle with Death himself.

Heracles's Death-defying Feats

THE DIALOGUE

1) HERACLES: Help me, Father Zeus.
(*Shouting his battle cry, Heracles forces the crazed killer to his knees. Although Death puts up a ferocious resistance, he is unable to free himself from Heracles's herculean grip.*)

2) ALCESTIS (*awakening*): Where am I? Oh, what a bad dream!
HERACLES (*to Death*): Go on! Get lost! You've forfeited your rights.
DEATH: All right, all right! I'll consent.

His next adventure took Heracles to the land of Lydia in Asia Minor, where Queen Omphale, rich and surpassingly beautiful, was waiting for the proper hero to come along and sweep her off her feet.

THE DIALOGUE

3) MESSENGER: Queen, the well-known hero Heracles has just arrived from Greece.
OMPHALE: Tell everyone to get ready to welcome him here at the palace.

4) OMPHALE (*to herself*): I'll get this hero Heracles to fight the Cyclops. If he defeats them, then maybe he can be my husband.

5) MESSENGER: Queen, Heracles won't come to the palace. He's gone off to fight the Cyclops and he intends to kill all of them.
OMPHALE (*to herself*): He seems to be a real hero!

Curiously enough, the battle between Heracles and the Cyclops, and several other details of the story, were never even mentioned by the classical authors. Here, as elsewhere, *Classic Comics* depart somewhat from tradition, which makes many scholars deplore the use of comic books for retelling ancient myths. But that doesn't stop the publishers of *Classic Comics*. Nor should it, for the medium is a particularly appropriate one for treating these subjects. Few art forms surviving today are so similar to the Homeric epic in dramatic pace and excitement; certainly *Classic Comics* come much closer to the Greek spirit than most dry, scholarly translations of the ancient stories do. And the twelve-year-old children who read them can readily identify with them, for they are as randy, boastful, and quarrelsome as the classical gods and heroes (who were themselves rather childish), and as unsophisticated as the illiterate warriors who first listened to the songs of the blind bard Homer.

The Birth of Athena

Then Zeus from his head, by himself
he produced Athene of the gray eyes
Great goddess, weariless,
waker of battle noise, leader of armies,
a goddess queen who delights in war cries,
onslaughts and battles.
　　　　　—from Theogony by Hesiod
　　　　　(Richmond Lattimore translation)

The birth of Athena, who sprang fully armed from the head of Zeus, has for ages been an inspiration to poets and artists, not to mention the creators of *Classic Comics*. Their version of the scene perhaps lacks a certain classic dignity, but it compensates for that by shedding new light on the practice of medicine in antiquity. The ancient sources fail to mention that the god of medicine, Aesclepius, assisted at the birth as a midwife. *Classic Comics* put him there, armed with a sledgehammer for cracking open Zeus's gravid head.

THE DIALOGUE

1) AESCLEPIUS: Fetch me a stool.
　　PLUTO: Hit him with all your might!
2) APOLLO: Wait! Let's have the music first. Come forth, muses, sing and dance.
3/4) THE MUSES: *Hurrah! Hurrah!*
　　　　　Zeus is giving birth
　　　　　To a great conception
　　　　　To bring health to everyone
　　　　　And pacify the angry elements.
　　　　　Oh, bright goddess,
　　　　　Born from her father's head, bright
　　　　　And strong when the people need
　　　　　Her help and salvation!